KU-413-990

The Cards Can't Lie

The Cards Can't Lie

Prophetic, Educational & Playing-Cards

BY ALICE HUTTON

JUPITER : LONDON

133.324

48998

First published in 1979 by
JUPITER BOOKS (LONDON) LIMITED
167 Hermitage Road, London N4 1LZ

Copyright © Jupiter Books (London) Limited 1979

ISBN 0 904041 97 2

Reprinted in 1983

Produced in Great Britain by
SHENVAL MARKETING LIMITED
South Road, Harlow, Essex

STOCKTON - BILLINGHAM

LIBRARY

TECHNICAL COLLEGE

Composed in 11pt Monotype Baskerville, Series 169,
by Ronset Limited, Darwen, Lancashire, and printed
and bound in Great Britain.

Contents

The Cards Can't Lie

Capped by a card, one of the characters from *Songes drôlatiques*, published in 1565 and wrongly attributed to Rabelais.

I

Mysterious Beginnings

N O O N E K N O W S T H E O R I G I N of playing-cards for certain. They were
probably brought to Europe from the Near East by the returning
Crusaders during the two centuries after A.D. 1100. It is known that the
soldiers of Godfrey of Bouillon, the Count from Luxembourg who was
the first King of Jerusalem, brought back the game of chess from the
First Crusade. Chess did not start in the Near East but is thought to
have begun in India in about the year 500, though it was played very
early in southern Africa, eastern Asia and Babylon – and the civilisations of Babylon began 6000 years ago. Cards are also, according to the
theories of some historians, thought to have originated in India.
Certainly from time immemorial a four-handed game was played in
Hindustan called *Chaturanga*. It was a dice game and it involved the
movement of mock armies. The word *Chaturanga* means, in fact, 'four
arms of the service' in an army, and in those days referred (in aristo-
cratic order) to troops on elephants, troops on horses, troops in chariots,
and troops on foot. *Chaturanga* was a game of chance. Chess is not, but
card games are. To deal an honestly-shuffled pack is to take on the
same sort of chance as to throw dice. Nowadays chance, because of its
association with irresponsible gambling, has an ugly or disapproving
ring about it. This is because invoking chance by gambling is supposed
to be bad, whilst invoking chance by getting up in the morning and
going out into the street is neutral, and invoking chance by praying
to your God that certain things may happen is often positively virtuous.

[9]

This point is made here because of the intimate connection between playing-cards and consulting the oracle, delivering a prophecy or having your fortune told, and this association is historic. Chess developed, in a progress that has not been determined, from a four-handed game of chance using four armies commanded by four kings into a two-handed game of skill using two armies commanded by two kings, but with a chief of staff more active than the king: this is the queen in modern chess, but it was a male vizier in the chess that was developed by the Persians and the Arabs, who would allow no status to a woman at all. The Arabic form of playing-cards, which was perpetuated in Spain, was not to have a queen among the court cards, but as is still found in some parts of Spain and Portugal only a King, Chevalier and Valet (or Varlet: hence our Knave). It was the Italians who introduced the Queen to the set.

So there is an association between chess and cards which has still not been satisfactorily defined. Both have a military basis. Both started with four 'armies', though in chess the number was diminished. Both have pawns, although in cards the pips denote a seniority of rank which does not now occur in chess: and the disconcertingly revolutionary rule of 'Aces high' which puts the single pip into omnipotence is a very old convention in card games.

It has been suggested that early Indian playing cards, which were round and small – some, still existing, are only an inch in diameter and are made of thin wood or ivory – were originally placed on the squares of a chess board. If the fundamental and joint origin of chess and cards could be proved to be – as has been seriously advanced – much earlier than the fifth century A.D., perhaps more than a thousand years earlier, there would be a more acceptable basis for the theory that the figures represented in playing-cards, which are much more varied than the conventional Kings, Queens and Knaves in medieval costume which have become standard in the packs used in northern Europe, referred to ancient frescoes in remote temples where seers withdrew to consult the oracles about future events. This theory has been developed from a study of the very ancient Tarot cards, familiarity with which had nowadays been notably revived by those interested in prophesying the future. Tarot cards are much more colourful than modern conventional playing-cards because they have thirty-eight pictorial images perceptibly allegorical of the main conditions and crises of human life. They will be fully described in this book. For the moment it is sufficient to have established that they have portrayed for many centuries

The Vizier of Swords, from a beautiful pack of
Hindustani cards painted on ivory.

qualities such as Power, Magic, Love, Justice, Evil, Fortitude, Death and a Stoic Gaiety which defies every assault of Fate. If any of these forces can be indicated as having an influence on one's immediate future, one is fortified by the assurance of a prophetic statement of what is to come.

In the olden days when people sought knowledge of the future from an oracle it was a common practice to cast down a loose bundle of arrows or sticks in a chamber where the walls and ceiling were covered with representations of the major forces governing the shape of one's life – pictures, in fact, which some historians believe correspond quite recognisably with the pictures on Tarot cards. The arrows which pointed to various pictures, and the number of arrows pointing to one particular picture, could be interpreted by the eye of an expert sooth-sayer to indicate the future of an individual enquirer. And it is this association with divination or prophecy that is said to be the basic purpose of cards. The games of chance were developed later, merely as games, which would be won or lost by chance. The fortune-telling aspect was always the original function.

The picture cards in the Tarot pack, the most ancient form of cards we now know in a systematised way, are called 'atouts', from a French word meaning cards superior to all others, which in modern English might be rendered as 'trumps' provided it were understood that atouts never vary – they are as permanently superior to others as a King is to a Ten. Because this is a confusing thought under modern conventions it is better to keep the old international name and call them 'atouts'.

The four suits of the Tarot pack are Swords, Cups, Coins and Batons, which in the earliest Tarot cards were presented as Swords, Cups, Rings and Wands. There is a logical progression not only from Rings to Coins but from Wands to Batons and on to Clubs, the suit in the northern European pack. The Batons began to be represented as powerful and ugly cudgels like the enormous club which Hercules cut in the valley of Nemea before he slew the Nemean lion, and which he was constantly pictured as carrying. The symbols of these Swords, Cups, Coins and Batons will be discussed in detail later. What must be mentioned immediately is that these four emblems are all associated with the Roman god Mercury who was particularly worshipped by the non-Roman Etruscans. Through him they were associated with the Greek god Hermes who was the antecedent of Mercury in Greek mythology, but who had different qualities from those which were attributed to Mercury in the Roman mythology. The association with

Hermes also entails an identification with the Egyptian god Thoth, the medium of divine wisdom who was also the magician of the Egyptian gods. Thoth in his turn derived from the Babylonian god Nebo, the arbiter of the fate of mankind.

There is also an extraordinary connection between the symbols of the Tarot suits and India. A sword, a cup, a ring and a baton are shown being held in the four hands of the ancient Hindustani god Ardhanari. This is a composite, even a hermaphrodite god, the right half being the male god Shiva and the left half the female goddess Devi (Durga). In a representation of this dual god, Shiva, with his sacred bull behind him, is shown holding in his two right hands a baton and a cup. Devi, with her associated tiger crouching behind her, holds in her two left hands a sword and a ring. A representation of another Indian god, Hanuman the god of the winds, shows him holding in four hands a sword, a cup, a ring and a sceptre.

This extremely close connection of the symbols of the Tarot pack with the emblems of ancient religions was not known in detail in the eighteenth century, when an antiquarian tried to link the history of playing-cards with an age far preceding the Crusades, and was very severely handled by the scholars of the time. Court de Gebelin, who had previously published studies on the subject, wrote in 1781 in his *Le monde primitif* (vol. viii, p. 265): 'Originally the twenty-two figures of the Atouts or emblem parts of the Tarots were painted on the walls of the temples, a fashion inherited from Biblical times, to enable the worshippers to recognise the sciences, arts or conditions represented by the figures and their attributes when it was wished to consult them.' He went on to point out what was not disputed, that rods or arrows were thrown in a loose bundle, and as they fell they would point to various figures on the wall. These arrows were marked with four different tokens dividing them into four 'suits'. The figures on the wall were stylisations of various crises or qualities of the game of life, and the twenty-two emblematic figures in the Tarot pack, backed by the sixteen court cards and with the numerical element of the forty pipped cards, proceeding from One to Ten in four suits, corresponded to these early temple indications of the abstracts in life – love, marriage, ambition, temperance, friendship, luck, hatred, despair, hope, success, death and resurrection – the whole presided over by the quirky, unpredictable leader of the pack, the writer on the tablet of fate, the god who delighted in promoting the unexpected, whom we have now somewhat diminished in majesty to make him the Joker in the pack.

[13]

The Joker, from a pack of Swedish cards used for the
old Cucu (gambling) game.

The central figure in the succession of gods who are, after more modern discoveries, recognised as linked in the symbolism of the Tarot suits, was the Greek Hermes. This mischievous, irreverent, trickster god was among the oldest and most primitive personifications in ancient Greece, though the myths made him a comparative newcomer to Olympus. His name literally means 'a cairn' and he was originally thought of as the daemon inhabiting a pile of stones, or later a single block of stone, set up by the wayside for magical purposes. Most often these magical motives were concerned with fertility – either of the land or the family. Hermes therefore became very nearly a phallic symbol, sometimes by the mere symbolism of the stone pillar, later being represented as a square milestone with a head carved at the top and no other anatomy except a phallus projecting from the middle height of the squared stone. When Greek mythology rather belatedly got to work to settle a genealogy on him he became not only a major god but an extremely fascinating character. Hermes, according to the stories gradually given credibility by the poets, was the son of Zeus, born after that amorous king of the gods had created man, and consequently was aware of comely mortal women whom he increasingly desired to seduce. Hermes was fathered by Zeus on Maia, the daughter of Atlas, and she gave birth to him in a cave in Arcadia. His mother laid him in swaddling clothes on a winnowing fan, but according to Homer he grew with astonishing speed. This may well have been Homer's sly joke at the speed of erection of a phallus, but the circumstance became an ineradicable part of the traditional life-story of Hermes.

Within a few hours of his birth Hermes was strong enough and cunning enough to slip out of his wrappings when his mother was not looking, and set out in search of adventure. He came to Pieria in Macedonia and spied Apollo tending a herd of very fine cows. Hermes decided to steal some of them. In order that Apollo should not read the foot-prints of the departing cows and catch up with him, he made shoes for the cattle out of bark, and tied the shoes on to the hooves of the cattle back to front. Then he drove off his spoil at dead of night. Apollo was deceived as planned by shoe-prints instead of hoof-marks, apparently converging on the meadow where the cattle had grazed but going no farther. He sought his cows in many parts, but could not find them. One myth said that ultimately, because Apollo had the gift of divination, he discovered what had happened and set out to find Hermes. Another story said that he offered a reward for the capture of the thief and the stolen cattle, and Silenus sent his satyrs ranging through the land to discover the thief and claim the reward. Now Hermes, when he reached the outside of the Arcadian cave where his distracted mother was awaiting him, had found a tortoise, killed it, and used the shell to make a lyre, and with this lyre he had made enchanting music which lulled his mother to sleep, after which he slipped back into his wrappings again as though he was a new-born babe. The satyrs who were searching for Hermes and the cattle were passing through Arcadia when they heard the strains of beautiful music that had never come to their ears before. A nymph at the mouth of the cave told them that a precocious child had recently been born there and she was nursing him. The boy was so gifted that he had already made a strange musical instrument of tortoise-shell with cow-gut. 'Where did he get the cow-gut?' asked the detective satyrs, and they noticed two hides forming a curtain to the cave. At this moment Apollo, using his own skill, had located the cave and came to the entrance. He, too, saw the hides and went inside. He woke up Maia and immediately accused her son of stealing the cows, which he insisted must be returned. Hermes, in his primitive cradle, was listening to the charge but pretended to be asleep. Maia indignantly pointed to the baby and asked how such an incredible charge could be made against him. But Apollo snatched up Hermes and took him to Olympus, where he formally accused the baby of the theft.

Zeus was unwilling to believe that his own baby son was a thief, and ridiculed the suggestion. But Apollo pressed the charge, and eventually Hermes had to admit it. 'It was only a little theft', he said in mitigation. 'I slaughtered just two of the cows and if you come with me you may have the remainder. I was hungry at the time and I had to eat something. But I was very dutiful. I cut up the carcases into twelve equal portions as a sacrifice to each of the twelve gods.'

'But there are only eleven gods', protested Apollo. Hermes bashfully lowered his eyes. 'You are forgetting me', he said, implicitly claiming for himself the twelfth seat on Olympus which was never afterwards disputed. 'And I was hungry, so I ate the sacrifice reserved for the twelfth god. I took no more than my share', he added virtuously. 'However, that's all over now, and if you come down with me I shall show you where the rest of your cows are, and you are welcome to them if you will drop the whole business. Least said, soonest mended.' The two gods returned to Arcadia and Hermes went into the cave to make a fuss of his mother. While she was not looking he explored with his hand under a sheepskin and made sure that an object he had hidden

[16]

there had not been discovered. But Apollo had seen the movement, and asked what he was groping for. Hermes pulled out the lyre, and sounding it with his plectrum, which he had also newly invented, he burst immediately into a captivating song in praise of Apollo, the most attractive, intelligent and generous of gods. Duly mollified, Apollo followed the singing Hermes to another spot on the mountain where Hermes had hidden the surviving cattle in a cave.

By this time Apollo was so enchanted with the lyre that he proposed a bargain. 'You keep the cattle, and give me the lyre', he suggested. 'Done!' agreed Hermes, and handed over the lyre and led his newly-acquired cattle out to graze. While they ate he passed the time by cutting reeds and making a shepherd's pipe on which he played another entrancing tune. 'I should dearly like that pipe', said Apollo. 'Give me that, and in return I shall give you my golden staff which I use for herding my cattle, and I shall make you the god of all herdsmen and shepherds.' Hermes objected. 'My pipe is worth more than that. Give me the art of foretelling the future as a makeweight and we can call it a deal.' 'That is not in my power,' said Apollo, 'but I will do the best I can do for you. I was taught the art of divination by three wise women who nursed me on Parnassus. You go to them, and they will teach you how to take auguries from pebbles. Now I can't do more; may I have that pipe?' Hermes agreed to this exchange, and Apollo said it was time to take his young companion back to Olympus. There, Apollo narrated all this complicated haggling to Zeus, who was affectionately impressed with his forward child. 'But from now on you must respect the rights of property,' he warned Hermes, 'and never tell any more lies. It seems to me that you are a very knowing and persuasive young god.' 'I can't help agreeing,' said Hermes, 'and it seems that my gifts ought to be put to good use. You should not find it difficult to assign me an official position on Olympus. I suggest that you make me your herald, with additional responsibility for the security of all the property of the gods. Don't you think that that would suit my talents, dear old pater? Naturally I shall never tell another lie, though I cannot guarantee that everything I say will be the whole truth.' 'I'm not asking the impossible', said Zeus indulgently. 'The position is yours, but your remit will cover other activities. I shall expect you to be responsible for making all treaties, and you will have to supervise the promotion of commerce and organise free and un-impeded passage for merchants and travellers on all the routes of the world.' 'It's a tall order,' observed Hermes, 'but naturally it is within my capabilities and I accept the commission. Now about my uniform, regalia, insignia, badge of office and all that, we must come to some agreement. I shall need proper respect. And there may be one or two other services you'll find I can render for you later.' Zeus gave Hermes a herald's staff dressed with white ribbons, an emblem which by decree and universal convention everyone treated with the deepest respect. Because he was to be out in all weathers Zeus gave him a travelling hat with a broad brim against the rain, and Hermes later acquired small wings on this hat. He had wings on his golden sandals and became an extremely mobile god. He immediately inaugurated himself with the gods who had preceded him on Olympus by teaching them how to make fire by twirling a stick rapidly in a wooden socket, another symbolic allusion to his phallic fire, and from that time on he was accepted without question.

Hermes busied himself with learning or inventing other accomplishments. The three nurses of Apollo to whom he had been recommended for a study of divination were in fact the rather shadowy figures of the three Muses – obscure because in later mythology they were numbered as nine and given names clearly identifying them. From the three primeval Muses Hermes learned how to foretell the future by casting pebbles into a bowl of water and observing the dancing curves with which they sank to the bottom. Later Hermes himself invented fortune-telling by throwing dice, and he also developed a sheer game of chance from the use of the dice – which originally were not neat cubes of bone or ivory, but knuckle bones salvaged after dinner. (It is interesting to note that in one of the earliest references to divination in folk-lore history it should be mentioned in a context also associated with gambling, like the use of cards). All the gods on Olympus agreed that Hermes, was fulfilling his duties as the herald of Zeus admirably, so that they were predisposed to agree when Hades put an extraordinary request to them. Hades was a brother of Zeus with Poseidon, and in the division of the world between the three sons of Cronos and Rhea, Poseidon had taken the sea, Zeus the earth, and Hades the nether world, the abode of the shades. But because people had a dread of pronouncing the name of the world of the dead they usually referred to Hades by the more flattering name of Pluto, the giver of wealth, in allusion to the gold and other riches which were mined from beneath the earth. Hades was anxious to lessen the dread of mortals for dying, and he had observed the tact and eloquence with which Hermes had discharged his duties as the herald of Zeus on earth. He therefore

Card designed by Jean de Dale and made in Lyon
around 1485.

requested that Hermes might act as his herald also, by taking the gold staff which Hades had previously carried for the purpose and laying it peacefully and persuasively on the eyes of the dying to summon them to the next world without fear. Because of this double role as herald, some confusion later arose about the staff with which he was depicted. The fluttering ribbons of the herald were later interpreted as snakes because of the association with the underworld, and eventually the conventional representation of this staff decorated it with snakes only. But the Wand or Baton which Mercury, as the later personification of Hermes, carried in Roman effigies and which was transferred to the Tarot cards as one of the suit symbols, is not the rod with the serpents twined to shape a lyre, but a sceptre which is more closely allied to the magician's wand with the additional echo of the symbolism of the gold staff which gently touched the eyelids of the dying and eased them into death.

The later attributions to Hermes, after he was credited with his skill in prophecy and his dual duties as herald, were that he was responsible for the composition of the alphabet and the musical scale, that he initiated the science of astronomy, a system of weights and measures, the rules of boxing and the disciplines of gymnastics. But already, in the evolution of the Greek pantheon of gods from the previous hierarchy of the Egyptian civilisation, he had absorbed some of the characteristics of Thoth, the god of intelligence and wisdom, and Anubis, the conductor of souls to the underworld. He became the god of eloquence, prudence and cunning, which could even go so far that he became the patron of fraud, perjury and theft, and as the protector of merchants and all who used the roads he was claimed – at least by the malefactors concerned – as the god of thieves.

His name was also borrowed in a comparatively modern revival of the cult of the Egyptian god Thoth under the name Hermes Trismegistus – a crude rendering of an Egyptian name meaning Thoth the Thrice-Great. To this god there were attributed the teachings of the Gnostics, a Greek sect living in Egypt who abandoned their newly-acquired Christianity even when St Paul was still alive, and by the third century A.D. had developed a theology of salvation through the revelation of hidden mystical secrets with a strong emphasis on magic. It was the magical connection that gave the later Gnostics their prestigious claim of the protection of the powerful necromantic god Mercury.

The Gnostics wilfully stole the name of Hermes/Mercury to give their new philosophy a more antique dignity. But the Etruscans who

[20]

took over the Roman/Greek god Mercury added more ancient dimensions. The Estruscans dominated Italy for centuries before the Christian era and were a serious threat to the growth of the infant civilisation of Rome. They combined extremely tough and dour qualities as colonials with – as can be judged from the wall-paintings in their tombs – a remarkably light and flippant approach to peace-time pleasures, particularly horse-racing, dancing and music. But they had a strong awe of the underworld and developed prophecy and augury to extremes of sophistication. The Romans learned sooth-saying from the Etruscans, and even when the older nation was no longer a military menace their augurs were considered supreme and were employed by the Romans in decisions of state affecting the whole empire, whether they were concerned with the interpretation of thunderbolts or with their particular speciality, prophecy through the examination of the livers of dissected birds. Hermes or Mercury was so fully adopted by the Etruscans that they gave him the native name of Turms, though most of the other Greek gods whom they recognised were known by their Attic names.

It is the attributes of the god Mercury, whose emblems were taken over unchanged into the suit symbols of playing-cards, and who had been the presiding genius over one branch of the art of divination through the wall-pictures which the Tarot atouts strongly resemble, that must be explored for the full significance of cards to be established – cards used exactly as Mercury's knuckle-bone dice had been used: first to penetrate the secrets of the future; second to make a semi-magic pastime out of an idle game of chance. (The latter being an accurate psycho-analytical description of gambling.)

The Knave of Swords, court card from an early
Italian tarot pack.

2

Leaves from the Book of Destiny

THE PRIMARY PURPOSE of cards was divination. Playing and gambling originated from that use. Propaganda and education were later applied to cards used for play. Prophetical cards bear designs corresponding to the master images of the circumstances of life which were found in ancient temples. To read them according to the emphasis suggested by pointing arrows or numbered pip cards is to try to determine what Fate holds for the future. Cards can be considered as unbound leaves which together make up the book of destiny. The god who was accredited with being 'The Writer in the Book of Destiny' was the deity who was known to successive civilisations as Nebo of the Babylonians, Thoth of the Egyptians, Hermes of the Greeks and Etruscans, Mercury of the Romans. The symbols of Mercury live on in the emblems of the suits of the pack. They are Swords, Cups, Coins and Batons. The *sword* had been a famous presentation to the god from his father in recognition of his intuitive and cheerful understanding. The *cup* was a relic of his apprenticeship on Olympus, when he had served as cupbearer to the gods until he gave up the post to Hebe, and he retained the chalice as his badge. The *coins* were what he was often depicted with as god of the merchants – he held a purse of netting and the coins could be seen within it. The *baton* was his herald's staff, and the golden rod with which he lightly touched the eyes of those about to die, also the magician's wand he held when his presiding genius over divination was being emphasised. In each of those four suits of cards there were, once the Queen had been admitted in the Middle Ages, fourteen cards: the King, Queen, Cavalier, Knave and ten pip cards. There were twenty-two atouts. These were dominated by the Fool, who was *hors concours* and had no particular value unless he was joined with a card of another value, in which case he omnipotently reinforced it. The atouts will be described in detail later, but it is relevant now to compare the role of the Fool, not with the modern Joker of whom he is obviously a direct ancestor, but with his originals in Greece and Rome, Hermes and Mercury.

Hermes was accorded regular festivals, as many other gods were, but because of gaps in the chronicles we do not know the details of most of the festivals. However, we do know that at the Hermaea (festivals of Hermes) in Crete, there was a ritual of what is clumsily called 'topsey-turveydom' where masters waited on their servants as they feasted. One is immediately reminded of the tradition still existing in the British Army by which the officers wait on the men during Christmas dinner, and there are other up-to-date instances of this. This has not been, like some so-called traditional customs, an arbitrary revival of a dead practice initiated by an enthusiast who over-rode the ossified resistance of his generation – a situation which is hard enough to credit of the British Army in any century. There has been a geniune tradition over 5000 years that in moments of extravagant celebration positions are reversed and the king waits on the page. This reached a peak in sixteenth-century England in the climax to the Twelve Days of Christmas where, on a relatively decent plane, the boy-bishop was appointed and performed certain sentimentally pleasing functions of ritual impression and liturgical nonentity, and, on a far more indecent plane, in the appointment of a Lord of Misrule, fully documented in the accounts of the orgiastic riots at St John's College, Oxford, where the most astounding 'topsey-turveydom' was performed. The Lord of Misrule was no more than a temporary exaggeration of the Court Fool, who was not merely allowed but encouraged to mimic his monarch to extremes of satire, often paid for by courtiers who had previously suffered the monarch's social lash, and so redress the balance of dissent against the behaviour of monarchists (rather than the monarchy). A role later entrusted to the B.B.C. and *Private Eye*. With these ancient attitudes Hermes or Mercury was always associated. His wit, his irreverence, his fundamental truth was always recognised and welcomed. And in this manner the Fool or the Joker throughout many

The Pope, an atout of an early Italian pack of tarots.

scores of centuries has been recognised not only as a comic relief but as a therapeutic necessity.

After the all-important Fool, the remaining twenty-one atouts followed in an order of precedence which has not always been the same. They are:

THE MAGICIAN.

THE PAPESS. For long she was called 'Pope Joan' because the (false) legend of a female Pope John VIII was especially well-known at the time when cards were becoming popular in Europe, but in more profound veneration she links with the High Priestess of ancient cults.

THE EMPRESS.

THE EMPEROR.

THE POPE.

THE LOVERS.

THE CHARIOT. This will be discussed in detail later but its immediate impact is to suggest the control which the charioteer possesses over his spirited horses.

JUSTICE.

THE HERMIT.

THE WHEEL OF FORTUNE.

FORTITUDE. In the Italian and French this card is called *La Forza*, *La Force*, and the implication throughout seems to favour strength of muscle rather than strength of spirit, for the traditional illustration on the card is of a woman holding open the jaws of a lion. She may of course, have had to call on fortitude in the modern sense in order to overcome her repugnance at coping with the saliva of a wild animal.

THE HANGED MAN. Far from being shocking, this is a rather whimsical image of a young man hanging upside down, tied by his right ankle to a wooden gibbet, his right leg jauntily scratching the back of his left knee, his hands bound behind him and a halo round his down-pointing head.

DEATH. In the Italian and French packs this card was generally unnamed. The image of the skeleton with the scythe lopping off the heads of all at its level was title enough.

TEMPERANCE. The connotation was, of course, in the times before the nineteenth century when temperance was twisted to mean teetotalism, a moderation in all indulgences.

THE DEVIL.

[26]

THE TOWER. On occasion this card was significantly (if Etruscan augury is remembered) named the Thunderbolt, and its conventional design was of a tower struck by lightning with victims being cast over the battlements.

THE STAR.

THE MOON.

THE SUN.

JUDGEMENT. The illustration here was the conventional image of the last day with the dead rising from their tombs for Judgement.

THE WORLD. This is a card of complex interpretation. Its traditional illustration was not always understood by later commentators. There was a figure, almost nude, with female breasts apparent but with the genitals obscured either by a veil or by carefully crossed legs. Because of the obvious breasts, the Victorians and others described it as a woman, but the original intention was to illustrate a hermaphrodite. Symbolic supporters at each corner of the card varied greatly in their message, but it was always concerned with an element of universality. They were the four winds, or the four seasons, or the four emblems of Mercury, or the four powers which ensured the stability of cosmic processes. Sometimes the hermaphrodite figure had its feet on a globe, like a juggler in a circus, to bring in the concept of the world. But in general the significance of this card, the last of the atouts, was of completion, wholeness, a harmonious end to the battle of life.

The Tarot pack of seventy-eight cards (forty pip cards and sixteen court cards in the suits, with twenty-two additional atouts) was traditionally called the Book of Thoth Hermes Trismegistus, and was claimed to contain reproductions of 'the parchment records kept in the Temple mentioned in the time of the eighteenth dynasty that were written on skins'. The eighteenth dynasty in Egypt, when Thoth was worshipped as king, began in about 1550 B.C., and there is no real evidence to link the card images with this period. But because false claims were made to emphasise ancient origins, there is no reason to reject all intimations of antiquity. There is fair ground for linking the playing-card images with the cult of Thoth Hermes Trismegistus, a parvenu faith of the first three centuries after Christ, which ambitiously tried to align itself with older Egyptian culture. The cult of Hermes Trismegistus genuinely derived from the reverence paid to the gods Nebo of the Babylonians, the Greek Hermes, the filtered concept of Thoth as it emerged in the year A.D. 50, and the strong cult of Mercury

Justice, an atout of an early Italian pack of tarots.

activated by the Etruscans and others in Italy. That is a sufficiently justifiable foundation on which to base the use of the images later put onto parchment, card or wood which are today substantiated in the use of playing-cards. Whether we use them today as toys or oracles, they were once part of the great cult of Mercury and the earlier human concepts of godhead which preceded the reverence of Mercury in the earlier civilisations of Babylon and Egypt. At this time the pictures and emblems we still handle were entirely understood and were regarded with the mixture of familiarity and awe which the most relaxed religious people of today extend to their own church, its furnishing, its symbolism and its priesthood. In the earlier times it was implicitly believed that only by a study and interpretation of the apparently random conjunction of emblems, suits, symbols and degrees of number could the wishes of the gods be made known to mortals through the medium of the priests of Mercury, Thoth or Nebo.

The Babylonian god Nebo was known to the ancient Jews and is indeed mentioned in the Bible. Nebo, Thoth and Hermes, were all reverenced as the patron gods of speech and its transmission on an intellectual plane. There is a notable emphasis in what has been recovered of the ritual on the theme that 'the gods gave speech to mankind'. Since this cannot have any reference to the development of actual speech, scholarly conjecture could only limit itself to the transmission of normally unperceived evidence through speech. It came to be believed that a priest connected with the cult either conceived, or was inspired with, the idea of communicating the wishes of the planets and of the animal and vegetable kingdoms as well as those of the patron to mankind through a tightly-organised system that had the temple of Thoth as its centre and the priests of Thoth as its interpreters. The power that this system would give to the genuinely scholarly men congregated in the vast palace of learning which the Temple of Thoth had become would be great, and would notably increase the prestige of the foundation. Before that time the ordinary people had been satisfied *faute de mieux* with much more simple means of consulting the wishes of the gods or accepting guide-lines on the character and fate of new-born children through the decrees which were written at the birth of each child on the tablet of fate by (or on behalf of) 'The Writer in the Book of Destiny' who was called Nebo, Hermes, Thoth or Mercury according to the civilisation which had at that time accepted the abiding culture. The practical means devised by the priest of Thoth which earned for his god the reputation of giving speech to mankind was

[29]

effected by decorating the walls of the temple with a series of pictures giving representations of the ancient gods along with graphic illustrations, allegories or personifications of virtues, vices, dangers, crises and attitudes which were the most critical by the measure of common experience of the battle of life.

These pictures on the walls could be consulted by the priests by casting on a central altar a handful of arrows, straws or rods, which were the necessary implements of the magic of the Egyptians – and indeed the rod was adopted by the Jews as an instrument of magic during their captivity in Egypt. An example of the dual use of the rod, being cast on an altar or used as a magician's wand, occurs in Chapter Seven of the Book of Exodus: 'And the Lord spake unto Moses and unto Aaron, saying "When Pharaoh shall speak unto you saying 'Shew a miracle for you' then thou shalt say unto Aaron: 'Take thy rod and cast it before Pharaoh, and it shall become a serpent.' " And Moses and Aaron went in unto Pharaoh, and they did so as the Lord had commanded: and Aaron cast down his rod before Pharaoh and before his servants, and it became a serpent. Then Pharaoh also called the wise men and the sorcerers: now the magicians of Egypt, they also did in like manner with their enchantments. For they cast down every man his rod, and they became serpents: but Aaron's rod swallowed up their rods . . . And the Lord said unto Moses "Say unto Aaron: 'Take thy rod and stretch out thine hand upon the waters of Egypt, upon their streams, upon their rivers, and upon their ponds, and upon all their pools of water, that they may become blood . . . ' " And Moses and Aaron did so, as the Lord commanded; and he lifted up the rod and smote the waters that were in the river, in the sight of Pharaoh and in the sight of his servants and all the waters that were in the river were turned to blood. And the fish that was in the river died; and the river stank, and the Egyptians could not drink of the water of the river; and there was blood throughout all the land of Egypt.'

In the temple of Thoth the rods of the priests fell on the altar and as they came to rest they pointed with varying emphasis of number towards the pictures on the walls. Since these pictures conventionally represented the major events in human life, their pattern of falling became the 'speech of the god' which was readily interpreted by the priests, confirming their premise that Thoth was the god of speech and his priests were the mouthpieces of the gods. This exaltation of the magic of speech went even as far as the sacrifice of tongues, a rite which continued into the time of the Roman emperors, when tongues were offered as one of the sacrifices to Mercury. As a development of consultations confined to the temple, the unbound leaves of the book of Thoth Hermes Trismegistus were made portable by reproducing them in smaller sizes than the frescoes on the temple walls. The priests or magicians could then carry a pack about with them so that any consultation room became in effect a temple. When the Christian Church began to assume substantial power it naturally fought hard against any future reference to the ancient gods, particularly to Mercury, whose cult was so widespread. Fortune-telling, as it was now styled, became a clandestine pursuit. Since primitive beliefs are not easily abolished even by an ecclesiastical ukase, superstitious people still retained a belief that they were receiving divine guidance when they were consulting the cards, and to an extent this continues today, though few who 'consult the cards' realise that they are continuing the old traditions which began with the worship of the god Nebo in Babylon, Thoth in Egypt, or Mercury in the Roman empire.

Divination by cards was not the only pursuit of the initiates who interpreted the oracles. For long these 'magicians' were men of wide culture conversant with much of the science and philosophy of the day. A study of the cults of Mercury shows that he was worshipped under many attributes besides his outstanding position as interpreter and messenger of the gods. Initiates to the Mercury cult learned a score of the arts and sciences which Thoth of Hermes were supposed to have invented, not only speech but music, painting, astronomy and agriculture – which had begun with the raising and nurture of beasts exemplified by Hermes as god of herdsmen and shepherds (an early specialisation of all nomad tribes) and developed into the culture of crops. The pictures on the walls of the temple of Thoth – generalisations of virtues and vices, joys and sorrows, health and death – were recognisable figures which could be distinguished by unlettered people and were instantly known and accepted when they became transferred to the surfaces of cards. The pictures on the Tarot cards, modified through centuries of European and Asian use, are still considered as conforming to the posture, decorations and attributes of the gods represented in Egyptian temples. Though this was a surmise with little substantiation when Court de Gebelin first advanced the visual connection two hundred years ago, subsequent discoveries in Babylonia and Egypt have satisfied many later researchers that the atout figures have an affinity with the designs of gods, sciences, arts and conditions which are known to have been painted on the walls of temples from Biblical times.

Just as a medium was declared necessary as a vehicle between the normal world and the spirit world when spiritualism began to be practised under modern 'rules' in the nineteenth century, the priests of Thoth declared that the contemplation of the figures on the temple walls was not sufficient in itself to establish communication with the gods, for the pictures themselves had no gift of tongues. The priests therefore added to the Book of Thoth a second volume delineating the method of consultation. In effect they took away from the ordinary people their traditional custom of consulting the gods through casting rods or arrows, sticks or straws, on the ground. This method had already been worked up to some degree of sophistication. The rods were marked with figures depicting a father, a mother, a child and a servant, and four emblems were also scratched on them so that they were divided into 'suits' exactly parallel to what is known now. These antecedents of court cards and suits had a long history of use in connection with the worship of the gods and divination. Ivory rods bearing these scratched devices have been found in the tomb of King Qa of the very first dynasty of the Egyptian kingdoms who was buried some 6000 years ago. These ancient divining arrows became the numbered or pip cards now in general use in the pack. They probably originated as simple rods comparable to those used by Aaron and the Egyptian sorcerers in Pharaoh's court, and in some parts of the great conglomerate of land stretching from Greece through Asia Minor to Assyria, where all our modern religions were born, there was a substitution of a quiver of arrows in place of the rods, or a bundle of straws as are known to have been used by the ancient Greeks during consultation of the oracle at Delphi.

When the wall-images were later disseminated and made portable by being reproduced on cards, the 'suit' markings evolved as the emblems denoting the four chief attributes of the god Mercury. These emblems can be seen reproduced on many of the ancient statues of Mercury that are still preserved in museums throughout the world. One important representation of Mercury (Hermes) is in his role as Argiphontes, the slayer of Argos; Argos was a many-eyed monster whom Hera, wife of Zeus, appointed to keep guard over Io, a maiden beloved by Zeus whom Hera had turned into a heifer to foil the seduction of her husband – but Zeus requested Hermes to kill Argos and the younger god did so with a sword specially presented to him by the

The Six of Rods, pip card from an early Italian tarot
pack.

The Valet of Cups, from a rare pack of forty-seven
German cards designed by Israel van Mecken, *c.* 1470.

king of the gods. It is this sword or *harpé* (literally a sickle) which Mercury is often depicted as carrying, and the Sword emblem became one of the four suit emblems of the divining rods and later the Tarot cards. Another common representation of Mercury is as Cyllenius, an allusion to Mount Cyllene where he was born to Maia in a cave. As Cyllenius or Agoneus he was considered the protector of merchants (and, by an unflattering declension, of thieves) and in statues commemorating this role he was shown holding a purse, through the network meshes of which coins were visible – and so the mark of the suit of Coins was devised. Probably the most frequent delineation of Mercury in statues and vase-engravings was as Caduceator, the messenger of the gods who bore the famous *caduceus*, the rod characteristic to Mercury. Without the ribbons (which later became serpents) the rod was a reminder of the god's magical powers of divination – and the bare rod, or Stave, (or, later, Club) became the third suit of the pack called Batons or Wands: in many old playing cards a pip card in this suit, the Nine of Wands for instance, showed a bundle of nine rods very similar to the original selection of sticks or quiver of arrows which was cast on to the altar for divination. A fourth guise in which Mercury appeared was as Chthonius, a reference to the Greek word for the soil with its suggestion of the underworld: here Mercury was playing his role of ushering souls into this world from the land of shades at birth, or conducting them out of it at death. The emblem selected for statues depicting him as Chthonius was not the gold rod of Hades, which could be confused with the *caduceus* or herald's rod, but the Cup of Fortune, a chalice shape which is still known in Italy as 'the cup of Hermes'. This beautiful shape was the inspiration of the form of the Etruscan funeral vases, one of the few surviving relics of Etruscan civilisation, and although these urns in their turn also derive from a use in Assyria, they have the dual reference to Mercury, who had once served as cup-bearer to the gods. This vessel was known as the Cup of Fortune because Mercury was reputed to hold it to the lips of mortals as an invitation to, or intimation of, a change in their fortunes, either joy or sorrow. And this, as the suit of Cups, makes the fourth suit in the Tarot pack. The connection of these ancient emblems with the cult of Mercury was more strongly established in the nineteenth century when the old Temple of Mercury at Baiae in Italy was investigated and, already in a poor state of preservation and rapidly weathering away, traces of the atout images were seen on the ceiling and all along the roof. It was concluded that this temple had been erected to Mercury by rich merchants of Rome in honour of him in his function as their patron god, and that the atout emblems denoting the crises of human life were painted on the ceiling instead of the custom maintained in the Temple of Thoth of placing them on the walls of alcoves and niches.

By some means the emblems of Mercury penetrated to India, unless the reverse was the case and these ancient universal signs had spread outwards from the Euphrates valley which was the cradle of all religions. The striking figure of the composite Indian god-goddess Ardhanari has already been mentioned. This deity has been described as 'the Isis of the Hindus, a pantheistic emblem typifying Nature, Truth and Religion'. The god holds in four hands the emblems of the cup, the ring, the sword and the rod. In India these emblems had achieved their own significance. 'They are recognised', said a nine-teenth-century commentator (William Hughes Willshire in his *Catalogue of Playing and Other Cards in the British Museum*, 1876, p. 62) 'as being the symbols of the four chief castes into which men were divided on the banks of the Nile and of the Ganges. Accordingly, the Cup denotes the sacerdotal rank, or priesthood; the Sword implies the king, a soldier or military type; the Circle or ring of eternity (that in the hands of the protector of commerce became Money) typifies the world or com-mercial community, and the Staff is emblematic of agriculture or the tiller of the soil.' As will be seen later, there were parallel but differing interpretations of these emblems when the symbols were widely circulated in Europe in the Middle Ages. In this close and largely unlettered world, visual emblems meant of course much more than the fanciful decorations of today's commercial logograms. A coat of arms on a knight's shield was not just a badge which his supporters could recognise, but often conveyed a precise message about his ancestry, even to the point of mentioning his bastardy if his father was sufficiently notable. Doctors of medicine carried, even into the eighteenth century, the wand which doctors had carried ever since they studied medicine in the multi-disciplinary learning of the pagan temples. It is the same ancient wand of Mercury and it still exists as the barber's pole – for the barbers were once barber-surgeons. Many vestiges of these ancient emblems and devices remain as conventional (and often unperceived) details on ordinary cards both in the Tarot and northern European packs.

Though the detailed history of the various systems of the packs will be given later, it may be noted now that the Tarot pack, known

Ace of Cups, from an early Italian tarot pack. The Suit of Cups derives from Mercury's Cup of Fortune.

in its country of origin Italy, as *Tarocchi*, has the seventy-eight cards which have been treated as the seminal form – twenty-two atouts and four suits of Swords, Cups, Coins and Batons with ten numbered cards and four court cards comprising King, Queen, Cavalier and Knave, and this pack is used in Spain and all the territories which have been influenced by Spain: Algiers, South and Central America, Cuba and Puerto Rico, and the Philippines. The Germans have a quite individually designed pack of fifty-two cards with suits called Acorns, Bells, Hearts and Leaves and only three court cards, all male: the King, Over Knave and Under Knave. France has a pack of fifty-two cards in the suits of Tiles, Pikes, Hearts and Trefoils (*Carreaux, Piques, Coeurs et Trifles*) which English and Americans know under their own names of Diamonds, Spades, Hearts and Clubs. Variations on all these packs exist in India, Persia, Sweden, and were formerly used in other countries such as Holland, which eventually complied with modern 'standardisation'.

Some of the blind reproductions of the ancient symbols occur in the Tarot packs and in the other packs which later derived from them, even though the smaller packs had been deprived of their most significant universal symbols. The Two of Coins had a girdle encircling the design, in memory of the girdle that Mercury stole from Venus – and in fortune-telling the Two of Coins has an association with theft which still derives from this ancient tale of a stolen girdle. On the Two of Bells in the German pack a pig was always depicted, and this is evidence – if evidence were needed – that the German arrangement derived from the *Tarocchi*, since this symbol was once on the Tarot emblems, the pig being sacred to Nebo. Later the pig was made sacred to Mercury, and pigs and tongues were always part of the sacrifice to the god at his annual festival. Moreover, both were sacred to Proserpine, whose descent to the underworld was celebrated on the day that, the lustful eye of the god Hades having rested on her, she was abducted from the arms of her mother Ceres and conducted to the embrace of the king of the world of shades by Mercury Chthonius, the messenger who called people home to the nether regions. On the Knave of Coins there is the design of a gazelle under a palm tree, a reference which dates back to the worship of Osiris, in whose pantheon Thoth played a major role. The Egyptian legend told how the gazelle gave a warning of the rising of the Nile by migrating away from its feeding grounds on the banks of the river to the distant desert, long before men had perceived the signs of the coming flood. The gazelle was thus a messenger of the gods to mankind and was made sacred to Thoth, whose person the Romans later merged into Mercury's.

The card which has come down to modern gamblers as the Joker represents all the nonchalant and cheeky skill of the original baby-god Hermes, all the irreverent satire and self-ridicule that the court jester exercised at the expense of the monarch he mimicked, and all the success that Mercury consistently achieved. In the Tarot atouts it is called the Fool. It has no number in the pack (all the other atouts having an order of precedence though there have been variations in this hierarchy over the ages). In the temple of Thoth the original of this image was not one of the pictures painted on the walls, but historians deduce that in all probability it was a statue in the centre of the temple which could be approached on an individual system by votives who had a particular problem and did not wish, as it were, a general forecast. The Fool has no number, yet it outranks all other cards, and is as volatile and undependable as Mercury himself. It controls and dominates every card in both the pip and atout sections of the pack. It represents the unforeseen, the unexpected, the uncertainty of fate which is a factor in all we do. The Fool is Destiny. The lucky irresponsibility of Hermes can always be discerned in its influence, and the element of irresponsibility, chance, and luck is of course a feature of all our lives. It is not only the self-defensive gambler who avers that the element of chance is indisputable as a governing feature of existence – and an unforeseeable feature save, possibly, through divination. Even the Darwinian law of 'the survival of the fittest' suggests that it is the lucky species who develop and endure, that of all the permutations of genes which can induce one effect or the other in succeeding generations it is the organism which by sheer chance has been endowed with the amalgam of genes which enables it best to meet the demands of the moment that survives – by chance, or the will of God, according to the theology of the moment. It was Napoleon who said that, whatever hard-sought qualities a general had equipped himself with, he still needed one other gift: good luck.

The twenty-two atout cards present allegorical figures in which the attitude, the costume, the accessories and the attributes each have a significance. That significance is not always now clear, but it offers a fascinating field of research because it derives from fundamental and primitive beliefs and associations which can be discerned in every civilisation. Some attributes are connected with the arts and crafts and sciences that were taught by the priests of Thoth and were later transmitted to disciples in Italy. Twelve of the atouts in their original form represent the twelve gods on Olympus, and others are connected with Egyptian gods or can be traced to far earlier mystical cults concerned with divination. When de Gebelin conjectured in 1773 that: 'The complete pack of Tarots, with pip and emblem cards together, were part of the Egyptian mysteries and particularly of the worship of Thoth', he was writing before the opening up of Egyptian antiquities in the great archaeological blooming of the nineteenth century. Only in the later epoch was it discovered that in the time of the eighteenth dynasty (that is, around 1500 B.C.) parchment records were framed in the temples of Thoth and these determined the laws. And if it were considered necessary to bring the laws to the full notice of the people this could be done by displaying pictorial symbols outside the temple. Thoth, it became known, used the stylus to write – strictly, at that time, to engrave letters on clay tablets – and this stylus became an emblem of Thoth as it had been of Nebo of Babylonia, so that there is good ground for believing that the stylus was the first form of the wand which became an emblem on the Tarot suit of that name. The sword which was later solely associated with Mercury was formerly also an emblem of Nebo. The purse of coins and the cup had always been associated with the mysteries of the three succeeding and merging gods of prophecy – Nebo, Thoth and Mercury. Astronomy and astrology were among the sciences and skills taught in the temple of Thoth, and many of the emblems associated with these pursuits are found among the Tarot atouts.

3

From Babylonia to Italy and China

WHEN THE WORD OF THE LORD God came unto the prophet Ezekiel, God spoke to him of two sister-whores of whom the younger was Aholibah, signifying Jerusalem. 'She was more corrupt in her inordinate love than [the elder sister], and in her whoredoms more than her sister in her whoredoms. She doted upon the Assyrians her neighbours, captains and rulers clothed most gorgeously, horsemen riding upon horses, all of them desirable young men. Then I saw that she was defiled, that they took both one way, and that she increased her whoredoms: *for when she saw men pourtrayed upon the wall, the images of the Chaldeans pourtrayed with vermilion, girdled with girdles upon their loins, exceeding in dyed attire upon their heads, all of them princes to look to, after the manner of the Babylonians of Chaldea, the land of their nativity:* and as soon as she saw them with her eyes, she doted upon them, and sent messengers unto them in Chaldea. And the Babylonians came to her into the bed of love, and they defiled her with their whoredom, and she was polluted with them, and her mind was alienated from them. So she discovered her whoredoms, and discovered her nakedness: then my mind was alienated from her, like as my mind was alienated from her sister. Yet she multiplied her whoredoms, in calling to remembrance the days of her youth, wherein she had played the harlot in the land of Egypt. For she doted upon their paramours, whose flesh is as the flesh of asses, and whose issue is like the issue of horses. Thus thou calledst to remembrance the lewdness of thy youth.'

Card from a tarot pack carved on wood at Besançon
at the beginning of the 19th century, but in the style
of wood-engraved cards of the 1750s.

This passage from the Bible not only expresses the deep hatred felt by the Israelites for their dangerously powerful neighbours the Babylonians and the Egyptians, but it also illustrates, in the words in italics, the common knowledge of the religious practice of the time, among other faiths than the Jewish, of decorating their temples with the images of 'men pourtrayed upon the wall'. Among these images in Babylon was the representation of the great Chaldean god Nebo, who also achieved a mention in the Bible when Isaiah spoke of him: 'Bel boweth down, Nebo stoopeth.' Nebo had a great and enduring influence upon the lives of the Assyrians and Babylonians. Modern decipherment of the cuneiform inscriptions of the time when he flourished show that the common people were taught by their priests to consult the prophecies of Nebo, who had inscribed at their birth what would befall each person during his or her life. Nebo was known under many ascriptions: the Illuminator; the god of the Sceptre; the god of Revelations. It is interesting in view of the later association with him of Mercury that Nebo's name in Assyrian signified 'Proclaimer Herald'. In the Babylonian tongue his name was slightly changed to Nabu. He was the son of the supreme god Merdach, as Hermes was the son of Zeus. He was the husband of Tashmit, whose name meant 'she who listens, intercedes, and reveals' and votives frequently appealed to her to intercede with her mighty husband to reveal what he had prophesied on the tablets of fate. Nebo possessed by inheritance from an ancestor god the craft of healing. Not only could he cure diseases but he presided at the peaks of human life, at birth and at death. His symbol was the sword, not because he was a god of war but because in his roles as herald and physician he first formally announced a state of war, and afterwards zealously tried to mitigate its consequences, for in those days the almost certain aftermath of war was pestilence. Nebo had the power of restoring the dead to life, the sick to health, and sinners to a state of grace. He was the source of all wisdom, the repository of all knowledge, the inventor of the art of writing which through the devoted labours of his priests had resulted in that most precious gift of history – the chronicles of different reigns, the records of the construction of buildings, accounts of the bravery and goodness of men – all preserved after the deaths of the protagonists as a permanent means of enlightenment for posterity. It is indeed posterity, the generations of the future, who ought to be most appreciative of the solid worth of his inspiration of recorded history. When the King Ram-man-nerari III built a great temple in Babylon eight centuries before the birth of Christ he raised a mighty

[43]

statue of Nebo with the inscription on the base: 'Ye who come after, place your trust in Nebo and in no other god.' Nebo was also the patron of agriculture who knew all the delicate details and observances for determining the best time to plant, to irrigate and to harvest. As messenger of the gods to earthly mortals one of his symbols was lightning. A hymn to Nebo translated from the cuneiform script of the Babylonians praises him as 'God without rival to Babylon, a nation without rival, whose weapon is the bloodless, breathless lightning, whose commands are as irresistible as the heavens where thou art supreme.'

The chief temple of Nebo was constructed at the town facing Babylon on the opposite side of the Euphrates which was named Borsippa but often referred to as Babylon II. The temple was called E-Zida, the true house. Innumerable tributes to Nebo have been found among the thousands of tablets inscribed for the King Ashur-banapal as part of the royal library. In the opulent language of the East he was praised as Mediator and Interpreter in opening the ears to understanding, Fountain of Sovereignty bestowing the sceptre on all Kings, Support of the World, Lord of All and Prophet of All. As the source of all science he was celebrated as the inventor of spoken language and of the art of writing, the great master of scientific learning and research. One of his most significant titles was the Speaker, not only because he had inspired all human communication but because as messenger of the gods his duty was to announce the fate of humankind. As messenger of the gods he bore the regal sceptre, sometimes portrayed as a conventional rod of office, sometimes as the staff with twisted serpents that was afterwards associated with Mercury, sometimes as a stylus, with which he actually recorded the destiny of humans, an instrument which was afterwards made the particular attribute of Thoth of the Egyptians. The twining serpents were directly copied from votive emblems which were a singularity of Babylonian worship, and they received extra force and significance in the Middle East after the development of the story of the rods of the Egyptian sorcerers being turned into serpents and swallowed by the serpent-rod of Aaron as has already been recounted in the passage from the book of Exodus. It was by the influence of this Babylonian symbol that the fluttering ribbons on the herald's rod of Hermes were afterwards changed to entwined serpents.

As God of Revelations whose teaching was conveyed through speech and writing, Nebo was particularly regarded as a soothsayer and

[44]

prophet. The Hebrew word for prophet is *nabi*, which has a clear connection with the root of the name of the Assyrian god. When cards came to Europe by way of Italy they were called *naibi* by the earliest Italian writers who mention them. In Spain cards were called *naypes* or *naipes* from their first introduction into that country. In Hindustani *naib* has the meaning of viceroy or overlord – 'Lord of All'. The Arabian divining arrows were always made from the tree called *nabaa*. All these indications suggest not only that divining cards (which later became playing cards) were derived from a system of worship of the Babylonian Nebo but also that they retained that name because of their pre-eminent association with prophecy as inherited from the cult of Nebo, 'The Writer on the Tablets of Fate'. The biblical association is also interesting. Not only were the prophets of the Old Testament called *nabi*, but the great viceroy and prophet Moses was recorded to have died on the mountain called Nebo which had in fact been dedicated to the god of the older cult. Nebo had in fact a dominating position in world theology and in the mirror of theology which came to be associated with the imagery of cards. His name was given to one of the planets – which we now know as Mercury. He was elevated to the great septemvirate of the principal gods of Babylon, along with what we now recognise as the deities of Jupiter, Mars, Venus, Saturn, the Sun and the Moon. The Sun, represented as a chariot drawn by horses, is the seventh card in the atouts of the ancient Tarot pack, and the Moon was originally represented by the horns which had been accorded to her with her Assyrian name *Nan-nar*, which meant the Heifer of Anu. This description came to her because the horns of a new moon resemble those of a cow. These horns achieved the significance of wisdom and prophecy and one of the most famous examples of the incidence of this imagery – apart from the design on the cards – is their use on Michelangelo's statue of Moses. In Babylon daily sacrifices were made to Nebo, the offerings including bulls, fish, birds, honey, wine, oil and cream. The wild boar was sacred to Nebo – as it was later to Mercury, to whom it was sacrificed and its commemoration is depicted on the Two of Bells of the German cards already mentioned. The boar was sacred among the Assyrians, and it was forbidden to eat its flesh on nominated days of the Babylonian calendar. Its ritual name was *Nin-shakh*, which had the meaning of Divine Messenger and this duplicated one of the titles of Nebo. All through the Babylonian territories statues to Nebo were erected. The annual ceremony at his great temple at Borsippa was an outstanding celebration in the year.

[45]

The most significant indication of the importance of the cult of Nebo is still familiar to us, though not often truly appreciated. The King Nebuchadnezzar adopted the name of the god as the first part of his own royal name, as his predecessor and his successor did also. It was an impressive mark of subservience. Nebuchadnezzar, who ruled from the year 605 B.C., threw himself entirely on the mercy of the god and invoked his protection by adopting his name, which had the meaning 'Oh, god, Nebo, protect my boundaries.' This was the climax of the increasing allegiance paid to Nebo, which had been surging for the last three centuries with a multiplication of temples in his name, dedicated variously to 'The Seer who guides all the gods', 'The Fount of Wisdom', and 'The Lord of Wisdom who guides the Stylus of the Scribes'. In the royal library instituted at Nineveh by King Ashurbanipal there is a tablet devoutly thanking Nebo for his guidance and for the inspiration which enabled the king to record his valiant deeds in writing which could thus be preserved for posterity. In the fluid warfare of the period the Assyrians invaded Egypt on a number of occasions and they too were over-run by the Egyptians, as were the Jews and the Persians. By this admixture of civilisations and from the intermarriage which accompanied it, not only the learning and the crafts and sciences of the individual cultures in the area became intermingled, but also their theology. By the time that Moses and Aaron were active in Egypt the Pharaoh of the time, King Menephthah, had established his capital at Thebes where the great temple of Thoth had been built. From this period Thoth and Nebo had been for all practical purposes merged into one god. And thus the Egyptians adopted the concept of a god who was 'The Writer on the Tablets' whom Nebuchadnezzar had glorified on one of his own tablets which still exists and after many thousands of years has been translated as 'Oh, Bearer of the Tablets of Fate, Oh, was 'The Writer on the Tablets' whom Nebuchadnezzar had glorified of heaven and earth, decree the length of my days. Write down posterity.' (The last sentence means 'Record in characters that cannot be deleted that I shall have children to succeed me.') There is a similar invocation on a colophon commanded by the king who was the father of Belshazzar. What is said by scholars to be the longest and most important of early Assyrian records, dating from 1100 B.C., is an inscription found under the foundations of a temple at Kileh Shergha, the ancient city of Asshur. This archive, a stem of papyrus covered with writing, eventually came to the British Museum. One sentence in the body of the text mentions divining rods being placed within the temple

[46]

as the 'oracles of the great divinities'. Many Assyrian tablets exist purporting to express in their cuneiform text the words which Nebo wrote, or commanded to be written, describing the virtues that men should strive to attain and there are others which define the evils to be avoided. One written prayer comes from a penitent who begged absolution by praying 'May the Tablet of my sins be destroyed' – a striking record of the belief of the times that Nebo controlled fate entirely, both when predicting the future and when making decisions concerning the conditions of life after death. This imagery of a tablet on which sins are written down may be recognised in the Bible. Moses prayed (Exodus 23: 32): 'Forgive their sins – and, if not, blot me, I pray thee, out of thy book which thou hast written.' Jesus told his disciples (Luke 10: 20): 'Rejoice, not that the spirits are subject unto you, but, rather, rejoice because your names are written in heaven.' And there is a passage in the Bible which is taken to be a direct reference to Nebo, the Heavenly Scribe, when the prophet says (in Ezekiel 9: 2): 'One man among them was clothed in linen, with a writer's inkhorn by his side.' This memorable passage describes a vision which came to Ezekiel in which he saw what were clearly the priests of a cult which believed both in sacrifice and in an acolyte who recorded the fate of men. The full passage reads: 'Behold, six men came from the way of the higher gate, which lieth toward the north, and every man a slaughter weapon in his hand; and one man among them was clothed with linen, with a writer's inkhorn by his side: and they went in, and stood beside the brasen altar. And the glory of the God of Israel was gone up from the cherub, whereupon he was, to the threshold of the house. And he called to the man clothed with linen, which had the writer's inkhorn by his side; and the Lord said unto him, "Go through the midst of the city, through the midst of Jerusalem, and set a mark upon the foreheads of the men that sigh and that cry for all the abominations that be done in the midst thereof." And to the other he said in mine hearing, "Go ye after him through the city, and smite: let not your eye spare, neither have ye pity: slay utterly old and young, both maids and little children, and women; but come not near any man on whom is the mark; and begin at my sanctuary." '

Ruthless slayer of the doomed, or indulgent preserver of those who had been marked by the gods of destiny to survive, Nebo was a god whose cult demanded attention, and possibly flattery. On one terracotta prism found at Nineveh a cuneiform inscription reads 'Oh, Hero Prince, Prudent Ruler, Oh, Nebo, Bearer of the Tablet of the Destiny of the Gods, Giver of Life, Prince of Babylon, Protector of the Living!'

This was perhaps the safest way to approach this omnipotence, and it was duplicated in the worship of the god who succeeded him in time and place and largely took over all his attributes. The Egyptian god Thoth still dominates the ruins of his mighty temple which lie outside the old capital of Thebes, to the north of the Valley of Kings. This temple was built or restored in the last years of the seventh century B.C., and dedicated to Thoth as the patron-god of literacy, communication and necromancy, the scribes and magician of the gods. The date of the building of this temple corresponds almost exactly to the reign of King Nebuchadnezzar in Babylon when the cult of Nebo was at its height in the eastern empire. But the infiltration of Nebo into the person of Thoth was not accomplished by military conquest, or any Assyrian coming down like a wolf on the fold. The reigning Pharaoh at this time was King Psammetchas, who succeeded in about 610 B.C. During his reign a new influence at court was established by Asiatic Greeks. The immediate consequence of this high-level immigration was that a cultural dam was broken between Egypt and Europe, not Egypt and Asia. Psammetchas displayed an over-riding enthusiasm for art, architecture and for foreign contact and commercial and intellectual adventure ... During his reign there was an important breakthrough in communication within Egypt following the intro-duction of a new writing-script which could be more easily learned and understood by the less educated, compared with the obscure and arcane symbols which had formerly been used – the so-called 'hieratic' writing only understood by the elite of the priesthood. This was a genuine advance, and it had been introduced by the priests of Thoth themselves in a most admirable surge of progress. But the priests sought no glory for themselves out of this innovation. They attributed it to their god himself, placing their works at the feet of their presiding genius and attributing their own decisions and discoveries to him. During the next epoch there was another cultural revolution, not this time concerned with Greece or the farther shores of Europe but with that other incubator of culture and religion, the region surrounding the valley of the Euphrates. It coincided with the stirring of the Roman civilisation, and ultimately there was an admixture of cultures. But for two hundred years culminating in the fourth century B.C. there was an Egyptian Renaissance of which a historian declared: 'Asia poured the fetid stream of her wonderful superstitions into Africa. The ex-orcisms of Thoth and the powers of witchcraft in league with him are

Character from a rare fantasy card-game, engraved on wood in the 18th century, produced at Lyon by Jean Rolichon.

The Cavalier of Rods, pip card from an early Italian
tarot pack.

the favourite themes which cover the polished surfaces of the monuments at this remarkable time.' From the viewpoint of an influence on the ancient world, the culture of Egypt had a far stronger instantaneous effect than the more remote rites and arts of Babylon. Nebo as a concept did not fail in strength. But most of his attributes were passed over, if they had not been already held by him, to Thoth; and it is the legendary influence of Thoth which was to inoculate Europe, even if the original message and inspiration came from the Euphrates. When the philosophy based on the divination of the Tablets came to Europe, with the building of a temple on the shores of the Bay of Naples, that temple was dedicated not to Nebo, but to Thoth – even if it was swiftly appropriated by Mercury.

Thoth and Nebo had similar heraldic emblems. They had parallel attributes. Both were declared to be the inventors of writing. Both were said to have the power of recording the fate of a human at his birth. Both presided over the judgement of souls after death. Nebo was called the Writer: Thoth was called the Scribe, and his most characteristic symbols were the stylus and the inkstand. Thoth had a month of the year dedicated to him, the first of the Egyptian calendar. Thoth carried a rod in many representations. A tablet at Wadi Magarah showed him bearing a sceptre in his right hand in a design strikingly similar to a figure in the Tarot pack. As would be expected from a god who had been allocated one of the months of the year, Thoth was numbered among the twelve great gods of Egypt. Many of them recall the generalisations which were afterwards common symbolism in the atouts of the Tarot pack. They were: *Num*, the creative mind; *Phthah*, the creative hand; *Maut*, matter; *Ra*, the Sun; *Khons*, the Moon; *Seb*, the Earth; *Khem*, the generative power in nature; *Nut*, the heavens; *Athor*, the nether world; *Thoth*, divine wisdom; *Ammon*, divine mystery; *Osiris*, divine goodness. Above this pantheon there was acknowledged to be one omnipotent god, but this band of twelve were the intermediaries. Thoth was recognised as the oracle and recorder of the wishes of the divine circle, and his most frequently drawn insignia was a palm branch or a stylus with a tablet, before the introduction of ink brought different mechanics to writing. He was also depicted on occasion with a crook-headed sceptre. His titles included Lord of Truth, God Twice Great – he did not become God Thrice-Great until the neo-Thothic worship of the Gnostics proclaiming Thoth Trismegistus – Great Chief in the Paths of the Dead, Lord of Divine Truth, and the Scribe of Truth.

Thoth was believed to be present at the birth of a child, when he noted the destiny that the gods intended for him, and more fearfully at death, when as arbitrator of the Balance of Souls he was present at the judgement. His sacred familiar was the ibis, the stork-like bird with a curved beak found in lakes and swamps and greatly venerated by the ancient Egyptians. Animals sacrificed to him included oxen, cows and geese. He had an office of close attendance on the kings, and there are many existing images of him showing him ministering to different kings, purifying them or inscribing their names on the sacred tree. At the judgement of the dead he presided over the balance that weighed their good actions against their misdeeds, and this significant part of his activities is commemorated in the figure of Justice among the Tarot atouts. Thoth was the intermediary who revealed the will of the gods to men. It was Thoth who composed the 'Ritual of the Dead', a moving document that is often found as a manual tucked into shrouds of mummies with his instructions on the etiquette required for the proper conduct of the soul in the world of the spirits. And Thoth had an aura of mercy and absolution when with his own hand he wrote in the world of shades the *Book of Respirations* ordained for those adjudged to have lived a good life, and who were given the book which gave them protection, sustenance and enlightenment, 'enabling them to breathe with the souls of the gods for ever and ever'. The god Thoth had three principal sacred colleges, situated at Thebes, Memphis, and Heliopolis, and king's daughters were gratified to serve as his priestesses. The wife of King Shafra who built the Second Pyramid is buried in a tomb at Sakkarah which records that she was a priestess of Thoth and her son was a sacred scribe. From this time in Egyptian history there were increasingly frequent representations of the scribes of Thoth, seated or squatting as they worked, holding a pen or a brush in the right hand and one or two spare instruments wedged behind the ear, with paper or palette grasped in the left hand.

King Cheops, who built the Great Pyramid, was a fervent devotee of Thoth, and had many pictures made on rock showing him in Thoth's company, with, in the king's hand, the Sacred Book which he himself had written for the furtherance of religion. As Nebuchadnezzar and other kings in Babylon had adopted the name of the god who meant so much to them, so did the Pharaohs seek to have the aura of the name of Thoth, and several called themselves Thothmes, meaning child of Thoth. It was Thothmes III who erected at the temple of Thoth at Heliopolis the two obelisks now known as Cleopatra's needles, which were later appropriated and sent to London and New York. The priests of Thoth were a hereditary caste, and an incredible claim was made that there was a direct line of descent from father to son over three hundred and forty-five generations – a religious dynasty which makes the papacy of Rome seem insignificant. As the officers who maintained the art of writing, the priests of Thoth were responsible for a number of books which, in pursuit of their traditional practice, they did not claim as individual authors, but universally ascribed the wisdom, the scientific compendia, and even the sheer light-hearted romance on occasion, to the all-inspiring Thoth. Of one great book of Thoth it was said: 'the man who knew a single page of this Hermetic book' – it is significant that the name of Hermes is here allied with Thoth's – 'could charm Heaven, the Earth, the Great Abyss, the Mountains and the Seas. Thoth enshrined this awe-inspiring work inside a box of gold, which he enclosed within a box of silver, and that within a box of ivory and ebony, and that within a box of bronze, and that within a box of iron: and he threw it into the Nile near the town of Coptos. But this secret act became known, and an eager search was made for the treasury of wisdom. Eventually it was located and recovered. But the man who found it, though he became a reposi-tory of arcane knowledge and a master of magical power, found that possession of the work always brought misfortune to him.'

Works of magic were, of course, one of the great specialisations of the votaries of the god Thoth. Magic was a valid force then, as it may still be, though nowadays more clandestinely accepted by pseudo-atheistic modes of thought. At that time and for long after, when people really believed in the divine Being – even if it were the wrong God by later standards – there was a far more resigned acceptance of fate, which had after all been inscribed on tablets at one's birth, and a far more unquestioning obedience to the priests who were intermediaries and interpreters of the great Thoth, who himself was but the intermediary and interpreter of the supreme and distant figure who was President of the Immortals. The people consulted priests at least as confidently as they now consult doctors. The priest would, after suitable ceremonies and divination, explain to the patient the instructions which Thoth had given to meet the present circumstances. He would record them on parchment, papyrus, or bark, and hang this prescription round the neck of the patient or perhaps within an amulet encircling the arm – purely as a reminder, though there was the inevitable reaction that this outcome of a magic consultation had magic and protective properties in itself. And as the purity of the art passed, the 'prescriptions' did become protective charms in themselves. One which has been preserved and translated reads: 'Thou art protected against the accidents of life. Thou art protected against a violent death. Thou art protected against fire. Thou escapest in Heaven and thou are not ruined upon Earth.' Such a comforting testament might well become a valuable insurance policy, well worth the selling or even the stealing, though by any strict consideration it was a personal analysis of the present standing of the fate of an individual which was only an excerpt from a record that had been set down immutably at the time of birth.

The most revealing Book of Thoth was the famous 'Ritual for the Dead', or the 'Revelation of Light to the Soul', which, as has been mentioned, was bound into the shrouds of mummies or placed in the sarcophagus. This manuscript was illustrated by pictures which, although they had previously to be explained by a priest for all their significance, still had a general value as representing an outlook, an artistic summing up of a creed, in just the same way as the pictures of the Tarot atouts today, though obscure and past skilful interpretation, convey a valid artistic message which makes a positive impression on us in this late century. Some versions of the 'Ritual of the Dead' are historically valuable because they express something of the philosophy of an age intermediate between ourselves and the original worship of Thoth, and roughly contemporary with the cult of Mercury which was supplanting the old liturgy and thought. These documents are the rituals ascribed to Thoth Hermes Trismegistus, a cult which has been shown to have originated in the Gnostic movement shortly after the death of Jesus. But the thought contained in them is not necessarily a revolutionary mirror of the philosophy of the first century A.D. Much tradition was still preserved, tradition which would have been forgotten if this intermediate and perhaps arbitrary reconstruction had been lost. There are three main chapters in the 'Ritual for the Dead', including a section of prayers and an exposition of the Creed. This is followed by further prayers, useful spells, and an exposition of what will happen at the actual Judgement in the Hall of the Two Truths. The dead soul is brought to the judgement seat, where Osiris, the personification of divine goodness, is on the principal throne. Around him sit forty-two assessors, each of whom speaks in turn from the bench to the suppliant soul, who is virtually on trial for his life among the shades. The particularisation of the kinds of innocence that had to be established throw a remarkable light on what was considered sinful at that time. The suppliant is required, for his future ease, to assure each assessor of his absence of guilt by declaiming these words: 'I have not blasphemed. I have not deceived. I have not stolen. I have not slain anyone. I have not been cruel. I have not caused disturbance. I have not been idle. I have not been indiscreetly curious. I have not multiplied words in speaking. I have struck no one. I have slandered no one. I have not eaten my heart through envy. I have not reviled the face of the king nor the face of my father. I have not made false accusations. I have not kept milk from the mouths of sucklings. I have not caused abortion. I have not ill-used my slaves. I have not killed sacred beasts. I have not defiled the river. I have not polluted myself. I have not taken the clothes of the dead.' According to the modern canon of sins, about the only acts which a man was absolved from defending himself from were adultery and card-playing. In all other respects it would appear that a summary of the 'good life' varied to a remarkably small degree over the scores of centuries during which particular aspects of morality have been preached.

The introduction of the cult of Thoth Hermes Trismegistus, which was the link between the assumption of power by the cult of Mercury and its subsequent transmission into the lore of cards, has left a comparatively large number of books which are not only useful summaries of contemporary knowledge and thought, but which also maintain a marked continuity from the teachings of the priests of the original cult of Thoth. Thoth was still accorded all tribute as a supreme teacher, and novelties in every branch of knowledge were still attributed to his inspiration and indeed fathered on him as the ultimate author. The works of Thoth treated of all manner of knowledge: basic theology, the educational myths of the creation of the world, and a considerable volume of astronomy and astrology, which at that time were a combined science. A series of astronomical statements of the weight of an encyclopaedia were translated from the Arabic into Norman-French a thousand years after Christ at the time of Manfred, King of Sicily, in whose realm was the most complete fusion of the philosophy of the Greeks, the Arabs and the later Egyptians: this work was called *The Aphorisms of Hermes*. Another work, entitled *The Cyranides of Trismegistus* dealt with magical power and the medicinal virtues of precious stones, of plants and of the portions of the flesh of animals. Works on chemistry and alchemy, including the inevitable investigation into making gold from baser metal, included *The Seven Seals of Hermes Trismegistus, Chemical Tinctures*, and the alchemist's vade-mecum, called *The Emerald Tablet*. But these were mainly secular works. The supremacy of Thoth Hermes

[55]

TOO2361

was passing. The secrets of divination were being passed to the personification of another god.

Though Mercury has a light-weight reputation today in the assessment of the virtues and dignity of the gods of Olympus, there was no god more honoured by the people of olden times, and no god more familiar, for he had his part, exercised his influence, or virtually demanded consultation in all the everyday matters of normal life besides the great climaxes of birth and death. He was a more 'comfortable' god than many, if only because he inspired less fear. As a messenger and aide to many of the more awesome gods he was never saddled by the people with responsibility for events in which he had been an active agent. Jupiter was a god to be treated circumspectly, for if his rage was fanned he might well despatch a thunderbolt to annihilate anyone who had treated him with contumely. If such a catastrophe did occur it would probably come about through Mercury acting as the lightning conductor, but the conductor was never apportioned any blame. Juno was a jealous matriarch, rather too staid for any warm sympathy on the part of humans. Yet she required scrupulous worship since part of her endowment as a goddess was the supervision of all childbirth. How fortunate, however, that when Juno assigned to Mercury the responsibility for actually delivering the new-born to the parents a much warmer and more humane influence permeated the care due to this critical peak in life. In the same way, Diana had appointed Mercury her lieutenant in many of the arts and crafts of life to which she was nominally patron, and it was easier and more natural to call on Mercury in an imprecation rather than go through the more solemn formality of a ritual approach to the rather remote Diana. In addition to all these roles as a deputy, Mercury retained, of course, his pre-eminence as the gentle guide into the land of death, the peacemaker and conciliator between disputing mortals, the intercessor who could be appealed to with a certainty that his orders could be received by mankind and accurately interpreted through the sign language developed for the priests of Mercury. When all these considerations were taken into account it was clear that Mercury was really more powerful than any other individual god, for although imposing and expensive sacrifices and ceremonies of propitiation could be instituted for the other gods, they could not reply to the invocations except through their messenger, Mercury. He was also directly responsible for the innovations of emblems, pictorial art and language through which direct approach could be made to him and he in turn

·JVPITER·

The Emperor in old tarot packs was often represented
by the god Jupiter, poised to dispense punishment
with a handful of thunderbolts.

RE DI DANARI

The King of Money, court card of the pip part of an
early Italian tarot pack.

could communicate his wishes by means of the divination expositions which are still now mirrored in the physical appearance of the Tarot atouts and the suits of the cards. It was a secret mystery, closely confined to the jealous priests of Mercury who were not slow to take revenge on any disclosure or unauthorised interpretation of the mysteries by initiates or renegade priests. For this reason there was little written record of the rites and no public presentation of the images until the destruction of two temples near Naples, which carried these emblems, compelled the priests to carry on their person the miniatures of these symbols necessary for the rites of Mercury – and so the packs of cards were introduced.

When the Roman state was flourishing Mercury was the most familiar god, the most everyday divinity, the power most frequently called on to help the human who was face to face with daily problems. He was a classless god, to the extent that the poor could resort to him by direct prayers and by priestly rites for which they had to scrape together their sparse coins. It is in the homes of the rich, however, that his traces can now best be seen, for the property and art of the rich were more frequently preserved. There were very few villas or mansions of the well-to-do Romans that did not carry a statue of Mercury enshrining one of his major attributes: as Caduceator, the bearer of news, of new tidings of inventions and discoveries, the doctor, the alchemist, the magician and the god with the stylus that wrote in the Book of Destiny; or as the god of commerce with the net purse visible in the hand of the statue and the coins discernible within – a very popular piece of art among the prosperous merchant class; or carrying the sword that marked not only the conqueror but the explorer, with exploration spreading beyond the discovery and military and commercial domination of new lands to the exploration implicit in the mind of man, the new ideas to which Mercury instrumentally gave birth through the spread of learning and the development of invention encouraged by the patron god of books and arts and sciences; or as the cup-bearer with the chalice from which mortals sipped their fate, the god who attended on birth and death and held the keys of Hades – a role most graphically portrayed by Mercury when he led Proserpine from the meadows of Sicily to the bride-chamber of the king of the underworld. Many of the most beautiful Etruscan vases still existing have the illustration of this gracefully sad tableau as Mercury conducts the reluctant Proserpine to the regions below. Others show the presence of Mercury at the time of death. There is a chased stone in the

[59]

British Museum showing a draped woman surrounded by her family as she prepares for death. Mercury waits behind the group, waiting to conduct the soul home. The cup of sacrifice is overturned, the tablet of Destiny is broken for there is no further use for it. It only remains for Mercury to guide the passing soul to the next world. Birth and death and love were the spheres of this god, for as the aide to Venus he was always active. No wonder, then, that Mercury was consulted at every turn of personal, emotional, commercial and intellectual life.

The merging of the attributes of the Egyptian god Thoth, (themselves derived from the Babylonian Nebo), with those of Mercury was most marked in Europe when a temple to Thoth was built and dedicated on the shores of the Bay of Naples. Already there was a group of temples to the great gods of Olympus at Baiae, some ten miles north of Naples. Of this group, the temple to Mercury remained in the best state of preservation into modern times. It was erected by wealthy merchants who had established villas in this area and were intent that the god of commerce who had clearly rewarded them so richly should neither go unhonoured or unobserved nor have an opportunity to change his attitude towards them. It was a practical insurance policy to venerate him. At the nearby town of Pozzuoli was the site of the temple of Thoth, where the mysteries of this god were taught by priests of the Egyptian cult. Here also, on the edge of the shore, there was a temple to Osiris, one of the twelve great Egyptian gods in company with Thoth, who was worshipped as that great manifestation of the supreme god which was demonstrated as divine goodness.

The purpose of the building of the temples to Egyptian gods was to serve the religious needs of the many Egyptians who now came regularly to Naples from Alexandria. They were in fact the merchants who accompanied the annual pacific armada that brought the imports of the corn harvest to Alexandria. Italy now depended greatly on the harvest of the Nile Delta to feed her population, and the Alexandrian corn fleet enjoyed special privileges and protection. It was the only foreign fleet allowed to sail between Capri and the Naples coast with topsails flying, and it was escorted by a convoy of war-galleys and greeted on arrival by a deputation of senators. The actual point of disembarkation was Pozzuoli, still a thriving and picturesque port. The great market of Pozzuoli displayed all the imported applied art of the East, carpets and wrought-iron and fine tools as well as the massive influx of food. The locality therefore became an international caravan-crossing where the learning and religion of other parts was discussed, explored and celebrated. The founding of the temples of the Egyptian gods was as significant a sign of the times as the building of the Mohammedan mosque in Regents Park in London in 1977. Osiris was worshipped in Pozzuoli under the alternative Egyptian name of Serapis, and the temple was called the Serapeon. It was buried by the sea during an extraordinary earth-slide in that volcanic area during the twelfth century, but four hundred years later, in 1538, it reappeared as the result of another great shift of the volcanic rock, and the straight marble columns of the temple once more emerged from the sea, riddled with the perforations of a species of small sea-snail that abounds in this area. Scholars who investigated the ruins of the temple placed its foundation at around 211 B.C., or possibly earlier. Between that date and a significant date some 350 years later the transference of the worship of the Egyptian gods to the Roman gods (who themselves derived from the Greek theology) can be definitively placed. For in A.D. 146 the Roman Emperor Antoninus Pius issued a decree ordaining that the worship of Mercury should be observed by the building of temples in Rome. This official act was merely an imperial recognition of the strength of a cult which had been strong for centuries, but clearly the centre of the cult as far as the Romans were concerned (the Etruscans having a less massive influence than the prosperous merchants based on the Bay of Naples) was the area around Pozzuoli and Baiae where the temples of Mercury, Thoth and Serapis had long existed. Antoninus Pius had in fact made a formal take-over of the attributes of Thoth and Serapis and combined them in the godhead of Mercury/Hermes.

Serapis was the god of commerce, and the Serapeon may well have been re-dedicated to Mercury long before the recognition by the Emperor. The other temple to Mercury at Baiae existed in a cluster of more native shrines and many of the emperors of the previous two hundred years – among them Caesar, Pompey and Augustus, had villas in the Baiae area, where the climate was not only refreshingly mild but there was an abundance of thermal springs to supply the baths with which the Romans indulged themselves wherever they could. It was a paradise of fashionable aristocracy and plutocracy, and the magnificent villas and water gardens which distinguished the spot were referred to by Horace in his poems. Of all the temples in this area, that to Mercury survived most successfully, its domed roof protecting it from volcanic ash in the series of eruptions which destroyed the other palaces and temples in the area. A long vaulted hall still stood, built entirely without windows, presumably to emphasise the awe of mysteries celebrated in deep gloom with the selective light of torches. These carefully placed lights would have revealed the oblong paintings on the ceiling which those who have seen them aver as strongly recalling the shapes and proportions of the figures in the Tarot atouts. The intervals at which those paintings which survive are placed are said to permit the accommodation of all twenty-two of the atouts known. The fact that the representations are painted on the ceiling and not on the wall has been taken to indicate that there was a slight diminution of 'mystery' in the rites as compared with those of more ancient times. In the Egyptian temples the figures intended as emblems of the virtues personified by the twelve gods, and the passions and fates and mortal circumstances which marked the lives of ordinary people were placed on the walls in recesses or alcoves where each had a separate dominance, like lady-chapels around the perimeter of a cathedral. But the fact that less exclusive presentations of the images were offered in some temples may be deduced from the biblical passage already quoted where 'the whore of Jerusalem', Aholibah, saw according to Ezekiel quite a company of 'men pourtrayed upon the wall'. It has been suggested that the priests of Mercury at Baiae placed their emblems of love and death, divine goodness and fate, together on the ceiling like a great picture book 'so that they might teach their followers the significance of the emblems when it was no longer worth while to make mysteries of them and conceal them'. But this theory does not accord with the almost total darkness of the original hall in which the paintings were mounted. Torches, of course, could be used, in modern terminology, either for spot-lighting or for flood-lighting. The atmosphere of a progressive penetration of the arcane would have been supported by the fact that even deeper in the temple, opening out of the main hall, was a 'holy of holies' containing the remains of an altar on which the traditional sacrifices to Mercury of tongues and the flesh of boars would be made at intervals and especially on the day assigned to him as his festival, the thirteenth day of May.

The genealogical descent from the Egyptians (and previously the Babylonians) of the later Mercury/Hermes figure has been closely argued by classical scholars who see in Hermes the personification of the Egyptian priesthood. It is proposed that Hermes, the genius who presided over science, and the conductor of souls to the other world, was regarded as the confidant of the gods because of the knowledge and trust he gained as their messenger and interpreter. The Egyptian system demanded strict service to this concept of messenger-in-terpreter – Thoth or Mercury – as a cult of perhaps the most intensely secret nature in all the history of religion. The priest-devotees customarily received no reward, passing-off all the glory of the task of presenting the god to humans as a charisma on the entire priesthood, redounding in turn back to the founder god, but also inexpressibly increasing the status and even self-importance of the priesthood. It was they who translated the otherwise unintelligible messages of the gods. It was they who passed on the learning which their god had encouraged them to research and compile. It was they who indeed spent much of their time in seeking or mutually transmitting knowledge so that a priestly college was to a great extent a university college. Equipped with this mastery of the sciences of the time, they were further fortified by their faith that they were a moral élite concerned with passing-on disciplines of learning and instructions on prudent behaviour in daily life, transmitted by their god to ordinary mortals by the intercession of the priests, who alone understood the painted or written signs. When commerce emerged as an important activity they annexed its patronage to maintain the influence of the priesthood on profitable business enterprises.

But there was a marked change in the character of the god when the Greeks took over many of his attributes for Hermes, and the civilisations in Italy later followed them. In Egypt, Thoth, though originally subsidiary to the supreme god and representing only one side of his functions, gradually grew in function and prestige until he was not only the guide of the dead but the father of spirits, godhead incarnate whose majesty was expressed in the abstracts of fire, which regenerates all things; light, the source of all knowledge; and water, the essential of fertility. When the Greeks developed Hermes as the guide of the dead and the interpreter of the gods they regressed to the more ancient idea that he was a god subsidiary to others more powerful than himself, and not an omnipotent being as the Egyptians had made him. The renewal of the concept of Mercury's omnipotence can be seen, as has been shown, when he was regarded, through his function as messenger, interpreter and aide, as being the most practical of the gods to deal with – an award of practical omnipotence. The Romans received Hermes from the Etruscans, for the worship had been introduced into Etruria by the Pelasgi in very ancient times, before the age of Homer. Hermes had been represented by a column, often the phallic column which has been mentioned. The Pelasgi first made him the god Terminus, who was represented also by a roadside column, and later by a pointing signpost, a very useful adjunct to a god who had the protection of travellers. When the Romans, who already knew of Terminus, became acquainted with the twelve great deities of the Athenians they adopted the Greek Hermes under the name of Mercury, assigned him the qualities of Terminus, and additionally concertina-ed old beliefs by giving Mercury the attributes of the Grecian Hermes and the Egyptian Thoth, who had an ambiguous position as truly omnipotent.

To get the best possible advantages from the worship of this god it was believed that it was necessary to approach him through his own priests, the only persons who were initiated into his mysteries and who could interpret them. These priests were already established in Italy through the foundation of the great temple of Serapeon. At Pozzuoli, therefore, there was developed a crystallisation of the cults of the various gods whose qualities had been absorbed from deities who had been conceived in many parts of the world. But this had not been the only out-spreading of the culture of the god. By some means his worship had gone east to India, and the primitive Greek beliefs about Hermes correspond closely not only to the qualities of the Babylonian Nebo but also to the legends which are still known about the ancient Indian Avatars. The Sword, Cup, Coin and Baton are borne by the composite hermaphrodite god who so strangely displays the emblems of Mercury still reproduced on the Tarot pack. And India is not the last link in the chain. Whatever the process by which the unbound leaves of the Book of Destiny were transformed into the relatively modern phenomenon of cards, the same transformation had taken place, earlier than it can be traced in any other region, in China. The earliest so-called 'playing-cards' which are known to modern researchers come from China. There is still a baffling gap of a thousand years of obscurity during which the evolution of portable cards cannot yet be traced, and it is during this long age that cards, like chess, really did acquire their use as playthings, a vehicle for games, a vehicle for gaming. But all through this mutation cards retained their function, which chess has lost, of divining the future.

4

Cards in the Orient and Southern Europe

THE EARLIEST KNOWN playing-cards are Chinese, but there exist cards in Korea which, though now not physically ancient, are believed to have existed in roughly their present form as an organised system of diversion – as a game – before the adoption of cards in China, and therefore the putative ancestors of the Korean cards would be the earliest known in the world. The Korean cards are used very occasionally for divining. The Korean national card game of *nyout* is played historically on one day a year for the purpose of foretelling the future, and elaborate rules are sold which detail all the names of every combination of throwing the cards 'according to the planets' and which curiously give these names in a language which is traced to races living in the mountains to the west of China: it is an indication of the spread of the use of cards possibly through India but more certainly from the confines of Mongolia. All Korean cards, though not now normally used for fortune-telling bear on their backs the sign of the arrow, a reference to the common primitive practice of throwing down a bundle of arrows to ascertain, by previously fashioned rules, what Fate has in store. The cards in Korea are strips of oiled paper measuring some seven and a half inches long by half an inch – as near to the shape of a stick or arrow as is practical when the cards are somewhat flimsy with the 'built-in obsolescence' of the paper medium. A Korean pack has eighty cards, ten in eight suits called Men, Fish, Crows, Pheasants, Antelopes, Stars, Rabbits and Horses. Chinese packs of cards vary, but some which are used today are representations of old Chinese paper money, with pictorial symbols of the old value. This paper money, some of which is still in existence, dates from the T'ang Dynasty which lasted for a period of 290 years ending in A.D. 908. The game played with money cards uses a pack of 120 cards – again fashioned as very narrow strips of cardboard – composed of three suits, but with each card appearing four times. That is, there are three suits of ten cards each, but these cards are quadruplicated. The three suits are Coins, Strings (of coins), and Myriads (of coins) and they are numbered from One to Nine, but there is an additional 'court' card to each suit although it does not bear the symbol of the suit. The top of Coins is a red flower, the top of Strings is a white flower, and the top of Myriads is called Old Thousand. In south China there are four suits: Coins, Strings, Mryiads and Tens of Myriads. But there are only court cards to the last two suits, making thirty-eight cards to the set, and again there is a fourfold multiplication so that there are 152 cards in a pack. Other cards in China are domino cards, which are used in virtually the same way as domino pieces but with much more elaborate decorations. In addition there are chess cards. A pack consists of four suits of twenty-eight cards with five extra jokers. Historical records show that cards existed in China at around the turn of the twelfth century A.D., which is just the time that Godfrey of Bouillon undertook the first Crusade, from which his soldiers are said to have returned with packs of cards and the knowledge of how to gamble with them, though no European cards of this date exist. Cards in Japan are not so firmly dated. They are tiny oblongs in packs of forty-eight divided into twelve suits called after the twelve flowers which are used as the names of the months in Japan. A suit shows the flower in four different stages of growth.

Indian cards have varied greatly through the ages. For long they were circular in shape, but oblong cards have been introduced within the last two centuries. The older cards had a set of eight or ten suits, with twelve cards to a suit, numbered One to Ten with two court cards. In a ten-suit pack one of the court cards of each suit shows a symbol of one of the ten incarnations of the god Vishnu, and the other court card portrays an incident connected with this particular incarnation. The suits were called Fish, Tortoises, Boars, Lions, Dwarfs, Axes, Arrows, Quoits (sometimes Cows), Shells, Swords (sometimes Horses). In other packs the suits include Swords, Bells, Coins, Flowers, Pagodas, Harps and other emblems. Swords and Coins are of course

The Three of Leaves, from a pack of unusually small
cards of the 17th century.

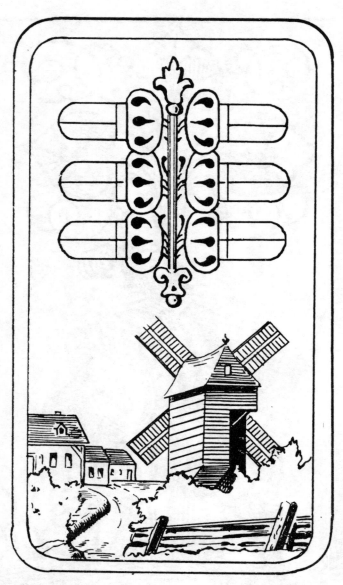

The Six of Acorns, from a pack of German gambling
cards.

suits in the Tarot pack, and Bells is a suit in the German pack, with Hearts, Leaves and Acorns. The most interesting set of Persian cards known are made of ivory and carry suit emblems of Turbans, Swords, Helmets and Crowns. It is interesting that Mohammed forbade the Moslems to play at cards, but the Persians are and always have been the keenest of card players. To them this is no sin because they belong to the Shiite sect of the Moslem religion which rejected the 7000 traditions of the Prophet. Yet the paradox with regard to Mohammedanism is that it is always assumed that it was the influence of the Saracens, the most severe Moslems of all, that introduced cards to southern Europe through the three avenues of trade with such ports as Venice and Naples. Also the influence of the returning Crusaders, who had picked up the game from the natives during foreign wars, and the very reverse of the Crusades, the invasion of Spain by the Saracens which is credibly suggested to be the occasion when the Saracens imported into Spain their own game of *naipes*, or 'prophets'.

Italy is regarded as the more likely spot for the introduction of cards, though not necessarily because the earliest definite date of the occurrence is quoted from there. It is a second-hand quotation, with no possibility of examining and testing the original. In a history of Viterbo written by Feliciano Busi and published in 1742 there is cited a statement by one Covelluzzo: '*Anno 1379, fu recato in Viterbo el gioco delle carte, che venne de Seracinia e chiamasi tra loro Naib.*' – In A.D. 1379 there was introduced into Viterbo the game of cards, which came from the land of the Saracens and by them is called *Naib. Naib* was in fact the term used for cards throughout many centuries in Italy, and its connection with the Spanish *naypes*, a corruption of the Arabic *nabi*, meaning 'a prophet' – with its own derivation from the name of the god Nebo which was recognised all over the near East – needs no great advocacy. But the date is not to be relied on as anywhere approaching the introduction of cards into southern Europe, only as the first surviving mention of the use of cards, and that not written at the time of the event. Covelluzzo's words, written in fact about a siege of Viterbo and nearly a century later in 1480 were, under the rubric A.D. 1379: 'There were encamped about Viterbo mercenary troops of the opposing armies of [the Popes] Clement VII and Urban VI, who committed depredations of all kinds and countless robberies throughout the Roman States. In this year of such great tribulation there was introduced into Viterbo the game of cards, which came from the land of the Saracens and by them is called *Naib*.' But this is merely a hint that it was the brutal and licentious soldiery who introduced this gambling diversion into the quiet city of Viterbo, which is highly probable. The year during which other, quieter, more cunning and almost certainly more prosperous speculative merchants – the true 'soldiers of Fortune' – introduced the combination of skill and chance which is gambling, possibly quieting both themselves and their wives at the same time with the assurance that they were in reality offering a sacrifice to Mercury which might have a beneficial outcome, and 'if you don't speculate you won't accumulate': this date has not been recorded. Certainly the Italians could not claim to be the originators of cards in Europe on this evidence alone. Only two years later there was a clear report that gambling was a well-known addiction in southern France. There exist the records of a commissioner of oaths in Marseilles named Laurent Aycardi. Under the year 1381 there is a record that a rich merchant's son, who had an addiction to card-playing, was about to set out on a commercial voyage to Alexandria. His friends voiced their fear that the voyage would prove so long and boring that he would surrender to his vice and lose all his money in gambling before he arrived at the distant port. Two of them therefore persuaded him to go to the notary, Aycardi, and promise on oath that he would not touch cards after his embarkation, not play at Alexandria, nor on the voyage home, nor even after he had landed at Marseilles again for at least a week. And for any infringement of the contract he would pay the sum of fifteen florins in gold. In effect, he was being bound over to refrain from card-playing in the sum of fifteen gold florins a time. There could be no stronger suggestion that the addiction to gambling at cards was already formidable in the south. Yet in the same period, in 1393, there is a written record of a warning to young men given by a moralist in Florence called Jean Morelli. Part of his homily included the caution: 'Don't play games of chance and don't play dice. Keep to the games which children play – *les osselets, les fers, les naibis.*' The last word is the standard rendering of 'cards'. If cards were known in Florence only as a children's game it seems that their conversion to real gaming had not yet happened there – but the passage raises a further query since it mentions 'knucklebones', which may well have been, as it continued for centuries, a children's game which was later called Jacks or Fivestones, but had still begun among the Roman soldiers as a gambling game of primitive dice.

Certainly cards were not used entirely for gaming or for divining the future. They had a role in education which will be enlarged on later,

[70]

The poverty of the middle classes in France, around
1650, inspired the series of *Proverbes* by Lagniet. Here
the vice of gambling at cards is attacked.

This card is part of the set known as the Mantegna
Tarot, one of the most beautiful examples of
Florentine engraving of the 15th century.

and illustrations on cards were being commissioned from reputable artists. The earliest engraved Italian cards which survive were too flimsy in texture to have endured shuffling and dealing, and much more greatly resemble the 'leaves from the Book of Destiny' which cards ars supposed to have originated as in their portable form. This is the famous set of the fifty Tarot cards of Mantegna, which are dated 1485. They were quite large – vertical oblongs some seven inches by four – and they were engraved and reproduced on strikingly thin paper. They represented fifty allegorical or mythological statements of the states of life, the arts and sciences, and the patrons of art and good living like the Muses, the Planets and the allegorical Virtues. They were executed by first-rate artists of the contemporary Florentine school although they come from the area of Venezia and the captions are in Venetian dialect. Historically they provide a very informative guide to the precedence then observed in the social scale, for the order of the first ten is the poverty-stricken Peasant, the serving Page, Artisans working on precious metal, the Merchant, the lordly Hunter, the Knight, the Doge, the King, the Emperor, the Pope. The delicate draughtsmanship with which they are represented is beautiful in the extreme and it excuses the attribution which used to be made that they were the work of Botticelli.

Individually painted Tarot cards still exist from an earlier date than these engravings. The exquisite Visconti Tarots were painted for the young Filippo Maria Visconti, Duke of Milan, in 1415 and his fee was fifteen hundred pieces of gold. The set was an enlarged Tarot pack with ninety-seven cards, the usual atouts being increased by representations of the Virtues, the Elements and the signs of the Zodiac. Duke Visconti played both games of diversion and games of hazard with this pack, the painting of which shows unparalleled workmanship, with the figures of gods and their emblematic beasts and birds. It was rare for such works of fine art to be executed for the personal use even of nobility or royalty. Thirty-nine years after they were done, in 1454, the Dauphin of France paid only fifteen francs for a pack of cards, which implies the use of some system of duplication, if not mass-production. There was a proliferation, too, of games that could be played with the cards. In the fifteenth century Francesco Fibbia, hereditary prince of Pisa but then exiled to Bologna, introduced the game of *Tarocchi*, or Bologna Tarots, in which some of the pip cards were eliminated and the pack consisted only of sixty-two cards. This game took the court by storm, and the delighted ruler of Bologna was privileged to place his coat of arms on the card of the Queen of Batons, and the arms of his wife, of the Bentivoglio family, on the Queen of Coins. With the spread of the popularity of card-playing there began the expected rumblings questioning the morality of the pursuit, but a first indulgent dictum declared that all games were permissible which did not cause people to stay away from Mass and which were an incitement to perform good works. Cards in the Tarot pack were therefore seen, because of their insistence on the popularisation of the virtues, the spiritual and lay establishment, and the healthy uncertainty of Fate, to have in some aspects a tendency towards morality. Within the next century the rules of three principal Tarot games were codified in a volume published in Venice. The acknowledged forms were the original Venetian Tarots with seventy-eight cards, the Bologna *Tarocchi* using sixty-two cards which was popular for centuries in Italy, and the Florentine *Minchiate* with the extra allegorical cards making a total of ninety-seven. Italian cards always differed from those used in other countries. They were bulkier and inflexible. The backs carried a design applied with a wood block depicting a flower or a coat of arms, and the edge-paper of the backs was folded over for a little distance on to the front, making a raised border of chequers which considerably increasd the thickness of the pack. In Venice this unhandiness was swiftly remedied by reducing the number in the pack. The atouts were eliminated as was also the Queen among the courts and the Three, Four, Five and Six of the pip cards. The resultant pack of thirty-six cards was used for the game of *Trappola*, a dangerously cut-throat gambling exercise which was always popular in Venice and was keenly taken up in Trieste, in Vienna and throughout Hungary – a land which emerged, like Persia, as another nation of dedicated gamblers. A slight variation was a diminution to a forty-card pack which was used for the Spanish game of *Ombre*, which was introduced into England by Queen Catherine of Braganza, the wife of Charles II, and became exceedingly popular during the next century. Catherine, a very devout Catholic, seems not to have been put out at all by any doubts about the morality of cards, and indeed they had been for the previous two hundred years perfectly acceptable to the Church. The artist Antonio di Cicognara, a famous miniaturist, painted an exquisite set of Tarots which he presented to Cardinal Sforza, Bishop of Pavia and Novara, and the Cardinal was so delighted with them that he requested the artist for similar packs for the use of his sisters, who were nuns in the Augustine Convent in Cremona.

[74]

The King of Cups, from an early Italian Trappola pack.

It was at one time thought to be certain that Spain had been the originator of the use of cards in Europe, since it was conjectured that they had been introduced, along with chess, by the Saracens, or Moors, who had penetrated into Spain from north Africa by A.D. 710 and were resident there, first as conquerors and then as a tolerated minority, until they were expelled in 1942. But there is no documentary evidence of this belief. The Moors now play *Ombre* (literally *El Hombre*, the Man) which is thought of as an old Spanish game but has a considerable similarity to the Indian game of *Ganjifa* and may quite credibly have a common origin with it. But the earliest surviving cards used in Spain date only from 1600. It is known, however, that from the fifteenth century the French towns of Tolouse and Thiers had a thriving manufacturing and exporting trade in making cards for the Spanish market. Others came from Limoges and Rouen, quite small in size – a little under three inches by one-and-five-eighths – and made in the Italian manner with the back edge-paper folded to form a border round the face of the card. The packs made for the Spanish market were almost exclusively designed for their national game of *Ombre*, and consisted of forty cards. The Eights, Nines and Tens were excluded and, following the Spanish tradition originated by the Moors, there was no Queen among the four court cards, her place being taken by a Caballero, or mounted knave. (But, as will be seen in the following passage from Pope, the chivalrous English restored the Queen when they adopted the game.) A peculiarity of the court cards is that in Italian packs the Kings are seated on thrones but in the Spanish packs they are standing, displaying flowing robes encrusted with jewels. Though the Spanish preserved the old emblems of Mercury for the suits – Swords, Cups, Coins and Batons, the Swords are straight and vertical two-edged rapiers and the 'wand' effect of the Batons is lost irretrievably in exchange for the great Herculean club with the knots of the branches protruding from the hefty limbs of trees from which they appear to be very roughly cut. *Ombre* is a three-handed game, and when it became popular in England little triangular card-tables were specially made for it, which can still be seen in some antique displays and are illustrated in many contemporary paintings and prints, including the work of Hogarth. Pope's famous description of his heroine Belinda sitting down to play at *Ombre* gives an exact and almost blow-by-blow account of the game, and the opening lines show how little the actual design of playing-cards has varied over the two hundred and fifty years since it was written:

[76]

Belinda now, whom thirst of Fame invites,
Burns to encounter two advent'rous Knights
At Ombre, singly to decide their doom,
And swells her breast with conquest yet to come.

Straight the three bands prepare in arms to join;
Each band the number of the sacred nine.
Soon as she spreads her hand, th'Aërial guard
Descend, and sit on each important card:
First Ariel perched upon a matadore,
Then each, according to the rank they bore;
For Sylphs, yet mindful of their antient race,
Are, as when women, wond'rous fond of place.

Behold, four Kings in majesty rever'd,
With hoary whiskers and a forky beard:
And four fair Queens, whose hands sustain a flower,
Th'expressive emblem of their softer power;
Four Knaves in garb succinct, a trusty band,
Caps on their heads, and halberds in their hand;
And party-colour'd troops, a shining train,
Drawn forth to combat on the velvet plain.

The skilful nymph reviews her force with care;
Let Spades be trumps, she said; and trumps they were.

Now move to war her sable matadores,
In show like leaders of the swarthy Moors.
Spadillia first, unconquerable lord!
Led off two captive trumps, and swept the board . . .

The poem goes on in a precise battle-communiqué the aptness of
which is only understood by connoisseurs of the game. At one crisis:

The hoary Majesty of Spades appears;
Puts forth one manly leg, to sight revealed;
The rest in many colour'd robe concealed . . .

And later:

The Baron now his Diamonds pours apace;
Th'embroider'd King who shows but half his face . . .

And:

The Knave of Diamonds tries his wily arts,
And wins (O shameful chance!) the Queen of Hearts . . .

[77]

The game of *ombre*, from a print in 'Seymour's
Compleat Gamester' 1734. Note the special three-
cornered table.

At which the King of Hearts (it is essential to know the rules for this ploy) takes a mourning revenge on the Ace of Hearts played from another hand:

> He springs to vengeance with an eager pace,
> And falls like thunder on the prostrate Ace.

And Belinda wins the game, as every reader knew she must!

LE MAT

The most important card in the tarot pack – The
Fool. Here a 16th century representation.

5

The Atouts and Suits of the Tarot Pack

THE GAME OF OMBRE began as 'The Man', a system of divination
based on the Tarot culture, and it is the nearest to the original
method of consultation that was reached in the utilisation of cards
north of the Mediterranean, save in Austria, until the modern re-
surgence of interest in the Tarot in recent years. Before we leave
consideration of southern Europe, therefore, it is convenient to set out
the significance of the detail and symbolism of the Tarot pack, which
is known to have had a committed following through the last nine
hundred years and is conjectured to relate to previous cults for possibly
two thousand years of obscurity and mystery. The twenty-two atouts
display between them illustrations of possible conditions affecting the
life of a man or a woman from the age of maturity. Much of human
life is here, in the symbols and significances and traditional interpretations that involve love, friendship, religion, uncertainty, luck, ambition,
opposition, enmity, good and bad luck, sickness, despair, hope and
death. There is a tradition in these symbols which appears to have
congealed in the Italy of the thirteenth century, which is the basis of
most of the costume shown, and yet there are declared to be signs,
positions, details of costume and attributes of interpretation which
hark back to an older tradition, not fully understood by the artists who
constructed what is really the matrix of the representations of the last
seven centuries, as if priests in a cult had commissioned particulars
of depiction which they did not fully explain. If a craftsman-artist

with no knowledge at all of Christian myth was instructed to paint the figure of a bearded man parting his ribs to expose a bleeding heart, he might be just as puzzled, and produce something just as crude, if striking, as an ill-informed artist commissioned to depict a man with his foot in the air – and producing a man suspended by one ankle from a gibbet: and we should all be making wild conjectures as to the real meaning of the Sacred Heart of Jesus.

The most important card in the Tarot pack is the Fool, and in his topsey-turvey world he may lead the atouts or follow at the end.

THE FOOL. This card is generally not numbered, or, if it is, it bears a zero. He is shown as a man in the garb of a court jester, with cap and bells, and with a staff over his shoulder bearing a bag or a bundle in the manner of Dick Whittington. He is depicted as a wanderer, young and lighthearted as the butterfly that often hovers over his head. In some packs he is naked, in others his dress is in tatters, and almost always there is a dog barking at his heels and tearing at his legs, as in old days the beasts were trained to behave towards vagabonds:

> Hark, hark, the dogs do bark
> The beggars are coming to town.

The diviners see in him all the qualities of Mercury himself in his various moods of suavity and jollity even when travelling under difficulties. There is in him an irresponsibility and an imperturbability based on inner confidence. This is youth at the beginning of the pilgrim's progress through life, not defenceless and not entirely unprovided for, since besides the equipment of his self-sufficiency he carries the prudent protection of the purse of Mercury in his hand. In play, this card dominates all others. In life, the Fool, if only he can keep his armour of youth, may dominate all opposition.

THE MAGICIAN. A young man is standing behind a table, on his head is a peculiar broad-brimmed hat, the edges of which curl, like an hour-glass on its side, into the mystic symbol for eternal life, which is the modern mathematical symbol for infinity and not unconnected with it. On the table are various articles and tools. One of them resembles a cobbler's awl, and the name of the card has sometimes been given as the Cobbler or Juggler. But the other articles on the table denote the emblems of Mercury, the Sword, Cup and Coin, while in his hand he lifts the Baton, which is the wand of the magician and the staff of

[82]

Mercury. If this is the young Fool on the first stage of his journey he has exchanged a certain sublime innocence for a more obtrusive arrogance. He has chosen the dangerous exploration of magic, and he has equipped himself with a surge of extra confidence which can lead to positive creativity – but in claiming an almost godlike control of the elements of the world has he, with equanimity, also lost his soul? This is youth in the first flush of responsibility, challenging his environment with a recklessness that may later have to be modified. There is an echo here of the initiation into manhood of the youths of primitive tribes who were sent out alone into the waste to find their god and also to find themselves. This magician may be making an offering, he may be making the first important request of the Keeper of the Record as to what life has in store for him. His hand is poised to lift one of the symbols from the table. Will he lift the soldier's sword, the cup of love and community, or the coin of the pursuit of profit? In primitive nations there is still a ceremony of placing a selection of articles before a youth in the belief that the one he picks up will influence the course of his life. In application to all the enquiries, of all ages, to whom this card falls as relevant, the Magician represents the use of the mind to affect the environment. There is a quality of indomitable searching about him. When it is presented upright it indicates intellectual strength and the bringing to birth of a fresh power to tackle the problems of the self. But when it is presented in reverse it emphasises the reverse side of the Magician's nature: the use of slickness and trickery to gain advantage over others, the fall into black magic and the grip of the forces of evil rather than the quest of harnessing the elements and the sciences for mortal good. It suggests an inability to summon up mental resources, a puny will that 'lets "I dare not" wait upon "I would" '.

THE PAPESS. The title of this card illustrates the changes in attitudes brought about by powerful folk-tales. Pope Joan, the woman pope, never existed, but she was confidently believed to have existed. The daughter of a missionary in Mainz who fell in love with a monk, she had the unusual twin attributes of an extraordinary capacity for physical passion with outstanding intellectual gifts, and exploited both by taking her young man off to Athens where she studied religion, philosophy, and eroticism until her lover died. She then went to Rome in the guise of a priest, became so striking a theologian that she was speedily promoted in the hierarchy and was ultimately elected Pope. But her other enthusiasm took temporary charge of her and she went to bed with a Cardinal. Some twenty months after she was made Pope John VIII, in 856 the falsified annals said, she was passing through Rome in procession when she suddenly went into labour. To the astonishment of her entourage and the even greater perplexity of the Roman bystanders she was promptly delivered of a boy, who was even more promptly claimed by the Devil in person, while she herself conveniently died on the spot. This story, often told, and readily believed (not out of particular irreligion but because the worldly excesses of the Papal Court at the time seemed to make it not impossible) became a classic myth of the Middle Ages. When the priests of the Tarot card community produced a symbol of a woman in high ecclesiastical office she was immediately assumed to be Pope Joan. In reality she was the symbol of the High Priestess of ancient rites and represented Isis of the Egyptians. She is signified by a female figure enthroned between two pillars with a curtain behind her indicating her temple. She is (naturally, in the eyes of the thirteenth-century artist) crowned with the triple tiara of the papacy and she has an open book on her lap. As the first female figure among the atouts she represents not only the priestess of Thoth but also Eve, the mother of all. During consultations about the future, if the enquirer was a woman this card was deemed to represent her in all future confrontations of cards, whereas it was the Magician who stood for a man. Court de Gebelin, who opened out the study of the Tarot in the light of his conviction that the origins lay in the worship of Thoth, declared that it had been the Italian cardmakers who had named the Papess and the Pope after the (to him) root names meaning Mother and Father, but the emblems of the Papess were Egyptian and her crown was the one borne by Isis in an Egyptian celebration of the reception by Isis of Osiris. These emblems which he mentions, not shown in all cards (even the old ones), include a crescent at her feet and a square cross on her breast which is not Christian but the more ancient Solar Cross. Instead of her hands holding a book on her lap they sometimes hold a scroll clearly marked 'Tora' and signifying the Secret Law. If the crown she is wearing is in fact intended to be that of Isis it signifies the regeneration of plants by the advent of spring and youth. The crescent at her feet aligns her with the Egyptian deity Hathor, who was the guide to the secret land (in some measure paralleling the function of Mercury) and whose protection was invoked for the dead and dying. According to the Ritual Instructions of the Golden Dawn, the high-priestess of the Tarot is 'the great feminine force controlling the very source of life, gathering into herself all the energising forces and holding them in solution until the time of release', and the twin pillars between which she is seated represent the positive and negative power on which the universe is founded 'unifying and absorbing the opposing energies'. According to other authorities the pillars represent Boaz and Jakin, the two columns of Solomon's Temple. It is clear from any interpretation, that the Papess, the first woman in the Tarot hierarchy, and significantly bearing the number Two in the order of the Tarots, represents the duality which harmonises aggressive singularity, and the feminine element in men which only the more modern psychologists have emphasised with any force. She is equilibrium but also fecundity, she represents a harmony between the heaving aspirations of the mundane will and the tug of eternity with its insistence that there is more at stake than the temporary triumphs of the present. In reverse she can be seen to stand for feminism unleashed, the transformation of a calm and divine wisdom into a reckless passion for gratification and fecundity, a symbolism which the purported career of Pope Joan does nothing to upset. Therefore when she is presented upright in the Tarot she gives a revelation of hidden reserves in the subject which will greatly fortify her, or to a man she may indicate the existence of a woman who will bring calm guidance to his life. To either sex she is a reminder of the force of intuition and an assurance of the creative potential, in art or in living. When presented in reverse she may emphasise in varying degree the absence of harmony and stability and the ruin that can bring. She is a warning of undue enslavement to passion or possession, and the folly of refusal to accept a balanced judgement from others on matters with which one is concerned on a plane of high personal and emotional involvement.

THE EMPRESS. A mature woman is depicted seated, sometimes on a throne amid all the trappings of power, sometimes in an orchard valley where all the fruits of the earth seem to issue from a horn of Ceres. She either holds or has at her feet a shield bearing the emblem of an eagle, or according to older styles a vulture, which was the emblem of the Egyptian goddess Maut, the divinity of Matter but particularly the goddess of maternity. In numerology her order of precedence among the atouts, number three, also signified childbirth and through childbirth harmony, by the extension of a sometimes tense duality into a third force which brings conflicts into oneness. The figure represents the deity of all the cultures, the Mother Goddess who is the source of all life. In her harmony she is passive, a state of being rather than a directive force. She is the warm emotion, not the fiery passion, the comforting breast of the mother rather than the mistress, the maturity of reconciliation and peace through experience of life rather than through the theories of the clever. In this golden maturity she has a significance to men as well as women, but the significance can be undesirable in the shape of over-emphasis on the protective security of the mother-figure. When the Empress is presented upright to the Tarot enquirer she indicates abundance, stability, the 'sensible' attitude, and to those who have fearfully denied themselves she is a reminder of the worth of human warmth and the practical advantages of a resilient foundation from which to launch to higher aspirations. When presented in reverse, she is the conventional mother-in-law instead of the mother: bitter, jealous, spitefully feminine, a tyrannous Empress.

THE EMPEROR. A crowned man sitting on a throne with menace. Curiously there is little sensation of sympathy created by any of the multitude of Emperors depicted on the Tarot cards through the ages until the end of the eighteenth century when artists felt freer to express human warmth within this subject. The costume and accoutrements of the Emperor vary greatly according to the period of the artist concerned. Those which seem to have been more ideologically commissioned do, however, hark back to Egypt. The Emperor seems always to be holding an orb, but the style of his sceptre varies. In one significant representation his sceptre is the *crux ansata*, the T-rod with a circle or oval above the 'T' which is the Egyptian *ankh* and is a common Egyptian symbol of power which is found on many a royal sarcophagus. Sometimes he holds between his knees a shield with the face device of an eagle. A frequent model for him is the assumed likeness of Frederick II, the Hohenstaufen King of Sicily who became the first great Holy Roman Emperor and remained a living force in the minds of such people as the thirteenth-century artists who designed the Tarot cards. The Emperor symbolises power, tenacity, ruthlessness. As a psychological father-figure he can represent both the merit and the unpleasantness implicit in that conception. Presented upright, he expresses male assertiveness and achievement, successful physical and creative effort, the rigour that is at some time necessary in all our lives. Presented in reverse, he is the idol with the feet of clay, the great statue of Ozymandias, King of Kings who cried 'Look on my works, ye mighty, and despair' – but who was encountered by the generations of the future as a horizontal core of a shifting sand-dune, a ruin in the solitude of the desert.

THE POPE. The robed Pope, wearing the triple crown and holding the triple cross, is seated between the two columns representing the temple, and his right hand has the two extended fingers that to the Middle Ages signified benediction: but often the pillars of the temple have Egyptian capitals, the sceptre with the triple cross is also associated unmistakably with the Egyptian symbolic rod which represents the recovery of Osiris, and the position of the extended fingers recalls the traditional sign which demanded silence within the Egyptian temples. Even the Italian pronunciation of his name, Papa, is ambitiously said to prove a connection with the Egyptian god Phthah. The symbolism of the figure of the Pope crystallises an orthodox reverence for the establishment. Presented upright, the card can indicate the virtues of authority, the teaching of experience, the revealer of the truth of God. Presented in reverse it denotes authority gone sour or tyrannous, unlawful power supported by false propaganda. There is no particular sanctity about the image of a Pope on a card. There is a negative aspect to his high position, and little spirituality in its positive presentation.

THE LOVERS. No association with the ancient cults of Babylon or Thebes can be determined from this card, which seems wholly to derive from mediaeval treatment of a sentimentalised Greek or Roman myth. A young man, in the doublet and hose of the time of the surge of Tarot representation, stands between two figures, generally female and supposed to represent Virtue and Vice, sometimes with the issue more pointed by making both figures naked and one of them a man. Above his head a buxom Cupid draws his bow to loose an arrow at a highly unnerving propinquity to the head of the youth. The young man stands as undecided as Paris at his judgement before Aphrodite made the improper suggestion to him that caused him to give her his vote for supreme beauty. The youth who set out on his pilgrim's progress is brought back to the thoughts of the Tarot enquirer as he strains to make his choice between good and evil, or, as other interpreters have ruled, between love for his mother and the loyalty claimed by his mate, or between the unthinking submission to the authority of parents and the past ranged against the cutting of hereditary allegiance in pursuit of a full and independent maturity – the decision which every young person must at some time make. As some of the diviners have ruled, the choice is not to be made by him, for the soaring figure of Cupid is about to make the decision for him, and it is not really the god of love but the youth's guardian angel. On this interpretation, the card when presented upright is an assurance that the right decision will be reached if natural emotions and intuitions are called into consideration rather than the poised arguments of the intellect. At any rate, a choice is to be made. Presented in reverse, the implication is that there is a danger of the choice being a bad one, or the danger very common both to young men as lovers, or older men as generals (or politicians) that they are unable to make up their minds to reach any clear choice at all. Life is not so simple as it was when the young man started out on his journey.

THE CHARIOT. This is the seventh card of the Tarot atouts, and by its number alone it has high significance. Pictorially it has produced some most memorable cards. A man is riding forward in a chariot. Sometimes he is the young man who is making his progression through the world. Sometimes he is a proud king, a conqueror standing at the reins in full armour, not always going into battle, occasionally riding in a parade of triumph with two queens in the car with him. The chariot may be drawn by horses, or by lions, or by oxen, or when the influence of the East is uppermost, by sphinxes. He may be the god of the sun or the god of war. Under the Egyptian influence he was taken to represent Osiris. In numerology the number seven is regarded as a prime number signifying unity within complexity and the number of occasions when seven has been cited – from the holy seventh day to the seven seals of the Book of Revelation almost passes notation. The symbolism of the card is based on forward progress. The man is proceeding in secure confidence along his path, shedding glory as he goes on all around him. It is a personification of control and achievement, but again in its negative aspect the achievement may be at the painful expense of others. Presented upright it indicates sure success, the reward of integrity and will. Presented in reverse its message is of the danger of forcefulness without consideration for others, the perils that follow self-centredness and human disregard.

JUSTICE. This is a formal figure in a most conventional pose of a stern

The Lovers, from a 15th century tarot pack. The young man stands poised between Virtue and Vice.

woman in a squared head-dress, seated on a throne and facing full forward like a judge confronting the condemned, a sword in one hand and a balance in the other. It is an unchanging symbol of law as accepted both in the Middle Ages, when Justice was summary, wilful and often brutal, and in the twentieth century, when they built the Old Bailey Central Criminal Court and crowned it with a statue, on the site of the most notorious prison in England. There is one variation in that the earliest Italian cards showing this design gave the woman the wings of an angel, and there is an interesting feature which recurs in the representations and is not usually pointed out. Because of the physical difficulty in holding a balance in one hand and to one side whilst seated, the woman is often shown with her (decently robed) legs open and her ankles crossed, allowing the balance space to sink between her legs rather than be brought to rest on her lap. But in most cases the artist, either wilfully or thoughtlessly, has drawn the balance so that its outer cup or pan – that is, the left-hand cup, since the balance is always held in the left hand – rests upon the left thigh so that it cannot sink any lower. In some instances it has come to rest on a raised thigh so that the right-hand cup has been forced down. There may therefore be a critical suggestion of fiddling present in the mind of the artist, though never in the thoughts of the earnest devotee who commissioned the original. Those who insist on an Egyptian origin for this mediaeval figure say that it represents the goddess Ma, the guardian of Truth, a title which was also claimed on behalf of the Pharaohs and of other gods. The nineteenth-century Egyptologist, Rawlinson, declared that 'The chief judge of every court is said to have worn an image of Ma round his neck, and when he decided a case he touched that litigant with it in whose favour the decision had been made, in order to testify that everything had been done with justice and truth. In the final judgement of Osiris the image of Ma was placed in the scale and weighed against the good actions of the dead.' This card dominates all the suit of Cups. Symbolically, like many of the cruder generalities, it can be used to bolster almost any platitude that occurs to the mind of the interpreter. When presented upright during consultation it can refer to abstract judgement, an impending act of judgement, or an implication that Truth has an important bearing on another card indicated. Presented in reverse, it can be a reference to injustice, the insolence of office and the law's delays, or maladministration and the financial ruin often incurred by all parties to a law suit, whether they are in the right or wrong.

THE HERMIT. A bent man, old and apparently joyless, cloaked and bearded with a staff in his hand, holds a lighted lantern high with his right hand like Diogenes looking for an 'honest man', or a storm-exhausted traveller at the end of his endurance. This melancholy figure, as the artists have made him, is an apparent contrast to the traditional attributes of the card, which is said to represent friendship, protection, love, safety, shelter, and refuge. This is not so remote from the subject of the allegory if the title is considered, but only seems irrelevant according to the drawing. A hermit lived in a hermitage, a retreat which had stability as well as solitude, and the hermit not only gave kind, if humble, charity to those who chanced to pass by and were in need, but also had considerable skill as a herbalist which was often called upon by travellers and by those in comparatively distant hamlets who would make the journey to consult him. The difficulty with the card is that there is no sense of repose in the figure at all. He seems to be at the crux of a journey under difficult conditions. This would accord with his status in a certain disposition of the atouts of the pack which was often used. If the Tarot atouts are laid out in correct order in a figure-of-eight design (the symbol for Eternal Life, but turned upright instead of horizontal) the Fool being placed first at the clock-wise beginning of the construction of the top circle – that is, at what military target directors would call 'seven o'clock' – then there is an interesting representation of the journey of life. The young man sets out, as gay as the Fool. He faces the world, faces it *outwards* since all the figures in this circle point outwards. He takes it on in battle (as the Magician), he encounters the powers and the establishment of the world (Papess, Empress, Emperor, Pope), he is faced with decisions between good and evil (Lovers) and continues strongly on his way (Chariot) not unmindful of mutual responsibilities between himself and others (Justice). At the point of the positioning of that card, the Hermit, he is almost full-circle at one stage of his life. He is about to cross over into another sphere which, as will be seen in the following cards, is far less concerned with *action against the world*, far more taken up with contemplation of the *forces within the self* and the attitudes and per-turbations that contemplation and meditation inspire. In this sense therefore the young man who set out gaily on the road to life is a *weather-beaten traveller*, apparently prematurely old and clearly buffeted by life. What all the interpreters have missed is that this is the man who is *about to be a hermit*, who has not yet reached the peace and stability of life, but is at this very moment making the journey to the spot where

[91]

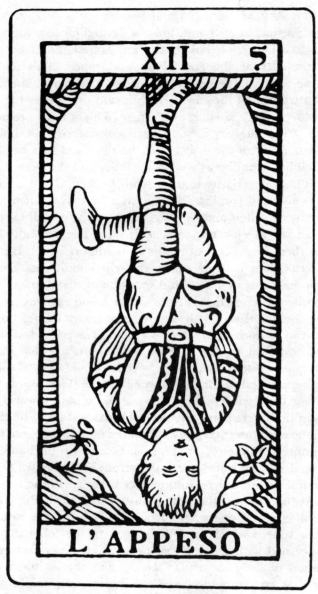

The Hanged Man, the most cryptic of tarot atouts.
This card is from an early Italian pack.

he will begin to contemplate its profundities. Presented upright in consultation, this card emphasises an immediate need to retire – not necessarily permanently – for consideration of the great problems of the moment. Good advice may come from another source or from the fruit of one's own reflection. Presented reversed, it refers to the refusal of advice, the perils of being headstrong, the stubbornness of not being willing to change one's course, which may seem like steadfastness but can in reality be fear of self and fear of novelty.

THE WHEEL OF FORTUNE. This indeed represents the crossroads of life. A most powerful symbol and one of the oldest allegories in the world. Over a suspended wheel, often shown as being turned by a monkey, the great Egyptian god Osiris, the husband of Isis, presides. Osiris is the judge of the souls of the dead, but here his concern is the fate of the living. Bound to the wheel, one going up and the other down, Anubis and Typhon strive to over-power each other. Anubis is an Egyptian divinity who was worshipped in the form of a human being with a dog's head, and was said to be an aide in conducting spirits to the judgement. Typhon, a monster of the primitive world, was described as a hurricane. He was the brother of Osiris and was said to have murdered him and cut his body into pieces and then to have thrown the remnants into the waters of the Nile. This strong card among the atouts shows these mighty forces striving to overcome each other on the wheel of Fortune, which inexorably turns, propelled by an animal, even if it is the highest intelligence below that of the humans. Often at the corners of this card there were shown the emblems of the four Evangelists, and sometimes the emblems of Mercury. In the Tarot pack the card has the general significance of a reminder that we must expect change and uncertainty in life. We are bound to the wheel and cannot escape until Osiris severs our bonds with his sword. The only freedom is the recognition of necessity: we must accept the trajectory of our destiny. Presented upright, the card indicates the beginning of a fresh sequence, a new turn of life, a solution to a problem, or a delayed reward for past virtue. Presented in reverse, it tells of the closing of a cycle, the need to summon up all reserves to meet a turn of fate which must be anticipated as unpleasant.

FORTITUDE. This comparatively flat allegory represents the second of the four Virtues personified in the Middle Ages. Justice has already appeared among the atouts and Temperance will follow, but the fourth,

Prudence, is omitted. The card shows a young woman effortlessly holding open the jaws of a powerful lion. The woman wears the broad-brimmed hat with its reference to eternal life. The young-man-turned-hermit in the withdrawn meditation of his later career must contemplate the development of that inner strength which overcomes animal force and primitive urges. The figure of the woman, especially the hat, conveys a reference to the Egyptian goddess Neith who wore an emblem on her head which was described as 'a shuttle'. The inscription on her shrine read: 'I am all that was, and is, and is to be. No mortal hath lifted my veil.' The last sentence refers to the marriage service among the Egyptians where, at the conclusion of the ceremony, the groom lifted the veil of the bride. The figure of Fortitude has this veil lifted, and in appropriate circumstances one of the meanings of the Tarot card is to indicate a bride. Presented upright, this card states that a calm morality will overcome primitive urges, that a serene courage will triumph over present difficulties, and reconciliation is possible either with a mortal enemy or forces within oneself. Presented in reverse, it implies defeat in the moral struggle, a deficiency of courage that will lead to capitulation in a moment of crisis.

THE HANGED MAN. A young man hangs upside down in the air, tied by his right ankle to the tree-trunk frame of a rough gibbet. He has his hands tied behind his back. His left leg is quite carelessly crossed so that the calf passes horizontally behind the right knee. The face is quite unconcerned and the head hangs down, sometimes into a pit, with the hair falling but sometimes with a halo encircling the head. This is the most cryptic of the Tarot atouts, and many different interpretations of it have been rendered. It is said that this form of hanging – not necessarily fatal but as uncomfortable and ridiculous as being placed in the stocks – was a form of punishment inflicted at one time in Etruria. It has also been added that the crossing of the legs in this fashion was once a secret sign by which Freemasons could recognise each other, but no one has ever said that they turned upside down to do it. Court de Gebelin in the eighteenth century illustrated a pack in which the man was in the same position, and even tied, but he was shown the right way up. From this note there has come the ingenious suggestion that the cult-devotee who originally commissioned the illustration in the thirteenth century wished to allegorise the 'missing' virtue of Prudence in the pack, and he used the Latin phrase that the artist was to show a man *pede suspenso*, meaning advancing cautiously with one foot poised off the ground as he decided where to plant it for the next step: but the artist read his brief as meaning 'suspended by the foot' and drew a design which appealed by its bizarre appearance to the devotees, who were perhaps glad of fabricating a mystery which they had no difficulty themselves in solving. Another interesting suggestion is that the figure is an allusion to the Roman god Vulcan, a being of great strength, which would be necessary for a long suspension of this sort, but also the god who was once thrown out of heaven and became permanently lame in one foot. In this aspect, the connection of Vulcan as god of fire may be alluded to in the illustrations of the man being suspended over a pit, where there is an uncomfortable lurking suspicion that there is a fire burning and the young man is being slowly roasted. The expression of complete calm on his face can be interpreted in a number of ways. If the whole composition is a reference to the pagan practice of annually hanging a god – or his substitute, such as the king – from a tree as a sacrifice to fertility, the victim may be expressing the inner content which has suffused many martyrs in the past. If the Hanged Man has deliberately cast himself down from the branch of the gibbet his radiant calm may denote that he was all the time assured of his safety because of the firmness of the knot of faith by which he had tied himself to the branch. If the card should really be read the other way up, there is every justification for an attitude of fearlessness because of the Prudence with which he is choosing his path. The consensus and general interpretation of this card has been that a knowledge of the laws of the universe, including the strength of hemp and the force of gravity is sufficient to produce true serenity. When the card is presented upright it refers to this inner knowledge which can defy apparently inevitable ruin because of a man's command of nature, courage and faith. In reverse it points to a rash reliance on knowledge not sufficiently assimilated, or the disaster that follows a foolhardy denial of reality.

DEATH. The thirteenth atout is Death, and that number has always been associated with extinction or disaster in Europe, though not for example among the Arabs, where it is seen as a symbol of order and organisation, so that in the view of some Death may not be so terrible, but the start of a new and perhaps more methodical system. The illustration shows the conventional skeleton with the scythe, lopping off the heads of a number of people which usually include the crowned heads of kings. When this symbol is used there is often the representation of a river, possibly the Styx, flowing behind, and a Babylonian pillar or a cenotaph-shaped column visible on the other side. But sometimes Death is shown as a rider on a white horse, and occasionally on a black horse. In the Tarot cards the message is that death is not the end: among the atouts the card occurs around the middle of the progression. But death is insurmountable: in one set of rules of *Tarocchi* the Fool is not supreme with the 'Joker's' powers he has according to other rules. The holder of the Fool takes back his stake, but the holder of Fortitude wins twice his stake, and if the trump of Death is dealt the holder ultimately sweeps the board, though not immediately – but it is eventually useless to oppose it. Yet people still struggle in spite of the card's assurance that death can be liberation into order. This is the principal message of the card when presented upright, though it does not deny that death may occur. Destructive death, however, is more 'in the cards' for those to whom the atout is presented in reverse. Apparently purposeless chance will most likely rob them of a person or possession highly prized.

TEMPERANCE. The third Virtue to be represented, Temperance is depicted as the figure of a woman equipped with wings who is pouring liquid from one vase into another. This is a conventional mediaeval allegory. It depicts the moderation and proportion necessary to make the correct compound from a mixture of ingredients. Sometimes the figure is shown with one foot in a pool of water with blue irises growing on the banks. Whether the symbolism has a Greek reference to Iris the goddess of the rainbow, where the correct alignment of the primary colours produces something of glory, or whether there is an Egyptian origin to this symbolism, it is clear that there is some oblation being made, since the pouring of wine and oil, or the mixing of wine and water as the preparation for an augury depending on the appearance of the streams in the mixture (as Hermes was taught to foretell the future by observing the dance of pebbles descending in a bowl of water) all have old connections with worship, reverence and divination through intercession to a god. Presented upright, this card instils the expected message of the need for careful control. In reverse it suggests that the bad handling of relationships will engender unnecessary strife.

THE DEVIL. Though the Middle Ages abounded in picturesque illustrations of the Devil, and many of the more conventional were

[96]

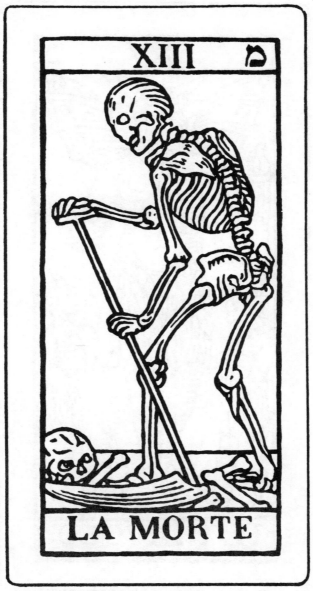

Death, the thirteenth atout. From an early Italian
pack of tarots.

The Devil, from an early Italian pack of tarots.

reproduced on versions of the Tarot atout devoted to him, it has been pointed out that in the older illustrations the genius of evil possesses many of the attributes of the Egyptian Typhon, the brother of Osiris, whose place on the Wheel of Fortune has been explained. One characteristic of Typhon was his long and leathery ears, and these appear on early cards. The Devil is represented as nude, with a loincloth, but with quite prominent breasts, and this suggestion of hermaphroditism in *all* devils, even the junior ones, is reinforced in a card of the seventeenth century showing the Devil with two minor devils with their hands bound behind their backs just above their tails and a rope passing round their necks and through a ring at the base of the Devil's plinth. The rope is carefully drawn to hide the genitals of these fiends also, but there is a strong suggestion that one is a woman though again both have comparatively pendulous breasts. In later cards two smaller naked figures of acknowledged sex as man and woman stand with unbound hands chained at the Devil's feet. It is possible to regard them as Adam and Eve after the Fall. Since a horned god was a being recognised in mythology before the literary creation of the Devil, there may well be an allusion to Pan in this allegory, and this would admit a more multi-toned interpretation of the occurrence of the card, since Pan was worshipped as the god of fertility and dispenser of life and abundance. When presented upright the card is interpreted as emphasising a need to subdue the baser self. In reverse it hints that matters have gone so far that the struggle may well be abandoned. But in reverse it can also bear the meaning that there is danger in an over-zealous denial of basic instincts.

THE TOWER. The formal illustration for this is of a tower of masonry struck by a thunderbolt with two people falling to the ground from its battlements and casements. The embattlemented top of the tower is always detached as though by an explosion and flames are roaring from the chimney so caused. The conventional explanation of the picture is that it represents the destruction of the Tower of Babylon – an interpretation that is sometimes aided by the fact that in the early eighteenth century the card is labelled *La Maison Dieu*, presumably in irony. But the Egyptologists have produced a far more striking reference which bears out the peculiar detail of the traditional card. The story was in fact told by the Greek historian Herodotus in the fifth century B.C. The Egyptian King Rameses II commanded that a tower should be built to contain his treasure and this was done. Rameses alone held the key. But still he found that items of his treasure were continually disappearing. He ordered that a discreet watch should be kept. The guards discovered that the architect had left a vital stone loose so that it could be prised open, and the two sons of the architect were making regular visits to the tower to exact their tax on the king's wealth. The wrath of Rameses blazed like a thunderbolt as he actually surprised the thieves in the commision of their crime. Knowing that they could expect no mercy, they threw themselves from the tower. As a result of this allied incident some writers have called the Tower the Castle of Pluto and made the story a warning to misers. But, although the story re-told by Herodotus seems undoubtedly the source of the representation of the two figures falling from the tower, there is another far more ancient reference of some significance. Dr Radau, an expert in Babylonian history, disclosed in his work *Miscellaneous Sumerian Texts from the Temple Library of Nippur* (p. 389) that the systematisation of the Babylonian religions was accomplished rather crudely by the king of the time with the help of the god whom he had decided to establish as the supreme deity, and with the aid of that 'son of the Supreme', the god Nebo – a name which will bear emphasis. The king's simple method was to destroy all rival temples. One of the tablets, translated from the Sumerian by Dr Radau was a *Lament of the Goddess Nin* who bewailed the destruction of her own and other temples: 'Great Nippur, and E-Kur and Ki-Ur with Girsu have perished in flame.' It is notable that there is no suggestion of fire in the story of the tower of Rameses told by Herodotus. But lightning strokes and thunderbolts were not only dramatic and highly illustrable events but were closely concerned with the divination of the wishes of the gods, and it would be a dull pack of cards that avoided the opportunity to treat of them. When presented to the enquirer in an upright position the Tower refers to the suffering of the individual through superior forces over which he has no control – an ancient answer to the constantly recurring plaint: 'If there is a God, why does he allow so-and-so to happen?' Presented in reverse, the card refers to unnecessary chaos and destruction, avoidable by a proper understanding of the truths of life and personality.

THE STAR. A fair young woman kneels naked and pours water from vases or shells held in either hand, sending it back into the pool or stream from which it had apparently been taken. In the oldest packs a gazelle stood beside her. Generally there was one tree in the middle distance.

The Tower, conventionally represents the destruction
of the Tower of Babylon. From an early Italian pack.

The Moon, .rom an early Italian tarot pack. Mystical
symbols give this atout a variety of meanings.

Always there were in the sky seven bright stars and one outstanding radiant planet or star – it was known by the French as *l'etoile flamboyante*. Those who bend more towards the Grecians say that the girl is Hebe, goddess of youth and cup-bearer to the gods of Olympus after Hermes, and that she typifies creation, song, speech, music, hope, immortality, eternal youth and beauty – but the items in the first half of this catalogue were in the domain of Hermes or Mercury. Those who favour the more ancient attributions say that she is not the Star, but Ishtar, the great Babylonian goddess, and that the flaming star is Mercury, the god of speech and transmitter of the wishes of the gods, or Nebo, 'The Writer on the Tablets of Fate'. The gazelle would certainly seem to have an Egyptian derivation in allusion to the gazelle which gave warning of the rising of the Nile and became the messenger of the gods particularly associated with Osiris. The card of the Star presented upright denotes the fulfilment of hope and the renewal of life, even of youth and beauty. Presented in reverse it is a denial of these promises, a declaration of rigidity and ageing and the neglect of opportunities.

THE MOON. A full moon casts its beams on a landscape framed by two strong towers. Two dogs, or sometimes a wolf and a dog, are howling at it. From a pool in the foreground a crayfish crawls to land. Drops of moisture are suspended in the air. The symbolism suggests the heretical beliefs of the Cathari sect who taught that after death the souls of the elect mount to heavenly bliss while souls of lesser worth are doomed to reincarnation in animals. The towers are the gates of Hell. The crayfish, a scavenger and unclean eater, will devour the dead. In its presentation, upright and reversed, this card only reinforces the obvious symbolism of its picture. Its deeper interpretation depends on its conjunction with other cards.

THE SUN. A naked child on a white horse holds a large red banner with the full sun behind and many sunflowers visible over a wall. Or instead of the child and the horse there are naked children dancing in a fairy ring, and sometimes two lovers hand-in-hand. Always there is the full serenity of the sun and droplets falling from its rays. The indications of this card include a proximity to the elements, precious stones and minerals; a happy marriage; prosperity; innovation and revival. Presented upright it foretells outstanding success against all odds and the vindication of reliance on daring invention. Presented in reverse it indicates failure through misjudgement, and unworthy success negated by the exposure of the mean methods which achieved it.

JUDGEMENT. Out of the heavens an angel sounds his trumpet, and the dead rise from their graves: a man, a woman and their child. Sometimes the man and the woman are rising from the sea, and only the child from the tomb. Again the message of the Death card is repeated. The traditional message of Judgement is not fear of the Last Day, but an indication of movement, regeneration, the creative impulse in man striving upwards towards the newly-exposed heights to which they raise their arms. Presented upright this card signifies joyful achievement and a new lease of life. Presented in reverse it is a reproach for lost opportunities.

THE WORLD. Within a vertical oval wreath a naked figure with flowing hair and a discreet loincloth dances with a wand in each hand. At the corners of the card are the symbols of the Evangelists which sometimes appear on the Wheel of Fortune. They are the Angel, the Eagle, the Lion and the Bull. The Angel signifies Knowledge, Mystery, Winter. The Eagle stands for Inspiration and Spring. The Ox represents Strength and Autumn. The Lion is Courage and Summer. All these symbols originally had significance in Babylon. The naked dancing figure, as has already been mentioned, is by tradition a hermaphrodite, for this is the end of the journey through life and all souls are joined in unity and the two sexes made one. The card signifies completion and wholeness, the climax and culmination, the full revolution of destiny. But presented in reverse it can only refer to failure.

In the suits of the Tarot pack the four court cards – King, Queen, Cavalier and Knave – dominate and control the pips of their own suits and play an important part wherever placed. Coins and Cups denote home and family life. Coins represent friends, strangers or partners, and Swords may mean any one of them, as the player wishes. But Swords and Batons are considered malign suits as against Cups and Coins. Batons represent enterprise and glory. Coins signify investments or commercial transactions. Cups stand for love and happiness. Swords involve hatred and misfortune. When dealing with the numbers, the first three will be called by their traditional names of Ace, Deuce and Trey. Ace comes from the Latin *as*, a small coin of the Romans. Deuce and Trey come from a mangled Franco-Spanish version of

[104]

Two and Three. The Ace, Deuce and Trey not unsurprisingly signify the beginning of a state or an enterprise. The Ace of Cups means the beginning of a love affair, the Deuce of Cups denotes opposition to it, the Trey announces consent. The same sequence with regard to a quarrel is followed, with the Ace of Swords signifying enmity, the Deuce that there is a reconciliation or truce, and the Trey declares open rupture or war. The Four, Five and Six, of each suit denote respectively inertia or inaction, opposition, and concentration in relation to the exercise to which thought is being devoted. The Sevens, Eights and Nines represent balance, poise or result. The Ten records uncertainty. Of the court cards the King stands for the man in any relationship, the Queen for the woman, the Cavalier for the child and the Knave for the servant. In a more abstract sense, outside family or personal considerations, the King stands for enterprise, the Queen for affection or love, the Cavalier for strength, conflict, rivalry, or hatred, and the Knave for a state of transition. The King of Batons is identified with a dark, kind friend. His Queen represents any friendly or charitable person. The Cavalier is dark and good. The Knave is a dark messenger or child. The King of Coins typifies a fair man who is friendly or at least neutral, and his Queen implies the same in the other sex. The Cavalier of Coins stands for strangers and the Knave brings messages or news. The King of Cups is a fair man and often represents a lawyer or adviser, lay or spiritual. The Queen of Cups is a blonde woman and if the man desiring information has a fair wife or sweetheart it is the Queen of Cups who stands for her. The Cavalier can be a fair-haired lover, and the Knave, besides portending news or messages can mean a child or even a birth. The Swords are an inimical lot to a man, and their arrival always augurs ill-luck. The King stands for a bad man, of dark complexion, a known enemy or someone who should henceforth be distrusted. The Queen represents a shrew, a gossip, a wicked or treacherous brunette. The Cavalier is a dark-complexioned enemy or perhaps a spy. The Knave is a sign of bad news, delay, or straight malice. All the Swords are indications of opposition arising outside the home.

EUGENE BOISSE.

Placard, engraved on wood, advertising a card-maker,
c. 1840. These placards marked the rise of this form
of publicity which had begun in the 16th century.

6

Cards in France and England

CARDS WERE INTRODUCED into France probably towards the end of the fourteenth century and almost certainly from Spain, having been brought back by soldiers of an expeditionary force. An edict of King Charles V in 1369 prohibited all games of chance and mentioned them in detail but did not name the game of cards. An edict by the Provost of Paris issued in 1397 forbade working people to play at 'tennis, bowls, dice, cards or ninepins on working days'. Nevertheless cards were in use at the French Court well before that time. There is a record of 1392 noting payment to an artist for ornamenting three packs of cards for the King. They may well have been in quiet circulation even before the 1369 edict. There is a mention in a manuscript romance of the 1330s, and a memoir by a former page to King Charles V mentions that he and his fellows were rebuked by the governor of the pages for playing at cards. A well-known print made in the second half of the fourteenth century actually shows the King (a fictional character in a romance) playing a four-handed game of cards with three attendants and two of the suits are visible as Coins and Batons. By the early fifteenth century the French had 'changed suits' and adopted the *Coeurs*, *Carreaux*, *Trèfles* and *Piques* which the British and Americans know as Hearts, Diamonds, Clubs and Spades. At about that time, too, the French began the custom of giving names to the court cards. There is a pack existing from 1440, for instance, where the four knaves are given the names of heroic knights such as Lancelot and Roland. These court cards continued for many centuries until, when Napoleon came to power, the new Emperor expressed a desire to institute a revolution in card-playing also, and he commanded that the old court cards should be re-designed to models of 'extreme elegance and purity' to replace the rash of rather vulgarly drawn philosophers and *sans-culottes* which had speedily been introduced once the hereditary King was guillotined. Some extremely beautiful designs were produced, but they found little favour among the actual players, and after 1813 a revised version of the old court cards was introduced and accepted.

The original French importation of cards from Spain did not spread to England until, as was the usual pattern, English soldiers engaged in the constant fighting in France from Normandy to Anjou and further south which characterised the fifteenth century, brought these toys back to their home country. English playing-card manufacturers immediately saw a chance to exploit the new craze. They were organised at a very early date. It was two centuries before they became important enough to be granted a Royal Charter by Charles I in 1628 to form the Worshipful Company of Makers of Playing-Cards as one of the Ancient Guilds of the City of London (which they still are today). But by 1463 they were sufficiently powerful to impose a monopoly, and a law was passed forbidding the importation of cards from abroad. By 1484 they had become a lively manifestation of the Christmas festivities, and in 1495 Henry VII passed the first of the many restrictive ordinances on card playing that became a feature of English domestic history by forbidding servants and apprentices to play at cards *except* during the Christmas holidays. Cards were of course permitted at court and among the leisured classes at any time they wished to play, and the kings of this land were frequently great gamblers. All the court cards at present in use retain the basic costume of the court of King Henry VII. As Catherine Perry Hargrave points out in her *History of Playing Cards and Bibliography of Cards and Gaming* (Dover Publications, New York, p. 170), 'The Queens wear the queer lappets over their ears which were worn by the ladies of Henry's court, but their way of wearing their crowns on the very backs of their heads did not come into vogue until Elizabeth's time. The Knaves with their flat caps, "broade on the crowne like the battlements of a house" are like the figures pictured in the paintings and tapestries of that far-off day, and their "striped stockings, red greene and yallowe" (Samuel Rowlands, *The Four Knaves*, London, 1611) are to be found on many an old figure in the early woodcuts. A "Knave" in those days was used in the same way as the French *valet*

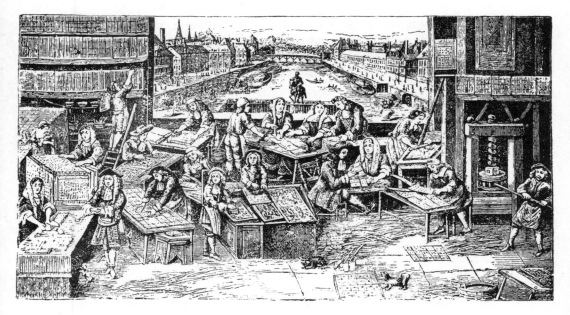

The workshop of a maker of playing-cards, *c.* 1690,
showing the processes of printing, stencilling, drying,
examining, packing and selling.

and merely meant "a son". Later it came to mean a rogue, and from that meaning our present term "Jack" is supposed to have come. Originally was "Jack a napes" which in its turn was from "Jack a naipes", *naipes* being the Spanish word for cards.'

In an England that was beginning to go Puritan in the early seventeenth century, either in spite of or because of the delight in card-playing indulged in by the Scottish King James I, propaganda against cards began to be virulent. An especial target was the use of cards for fortune-telling which was naturally widespread. A broadsheet entitled '*How Maister Hobson Baited the Devil with a Dog*' is a characteristic example. It recounts:

Nor far from Maister Hobson's house there dwelled one of the cunning men, otherwise called fortune tellers, such cozening companions as at this day by their crafts make simple women believe how they can tell what husband they shall have, how many children, how many sweethearts, and such like: if goods be stole, who has them, with promise to help them to their losses again: with many other like deceitful illusions. To this wise man (as some terms him) goes Maister Hobson, not to reap any benefit by his crafty cunning, but to make a jest and trial of his experience. So, causing one of his servants to lead a mastiff dog after him, staying at the cunning man's door with the dog in his hand, up goes Maister Hobson to the wise man requesting his skill, for he had lost ten pound lately taken from him by thieves, but when and how he knew not well. The cunning man, knowing Maister Hobson to be one of his neighbours and a man of good reputation, fell (as he made show) to conjuring and casting figures, and after a few words of incantation, as his common use was, he took a very large fair looking glass, and bade Maister Hobson to look in the same, but not to cast his eyes backward in any case; the which he did and saw therein the picture of a huge and large ox with two broad horns on his head, the which was no otherwise but (as he had often deceitfully showed to others) a cozening fellow like the cunning man himself, clothed in an ox-hide, which fellow he maintained as his servant to blind the people's eyes withal, and to make them believe he could show them the Devil at his pleasure in a glass. This vision Maister Hobson perceiving, and guessing at the knavery thereof, gave a whistle for his dog, which then stayed below at the door in his man's keeping, which whistle being no sooner heard but the dog ran upstairs to his maister as he had been mad, and presently fastened upon the poor fellow in the ox-hide, and so tore him as it was pitiful to see. The cunning man cried: 'For the passion of God, take off your dog.' 'No,' quoth Maister Hobson, 'let the Devil and the dog fight: venture thou the Devil and I will venture my dog.' To conclude, the ox-hide was torn from the fellow's back, and so their knaveries were discovered, and their cunning shifts laid open to the world.

But occasional bouts of horse-play like this did not stop divination by cards or any other means. A fortune-telling series of cards still exists which was published in 1665. The pack has two cards of explanation enclosed with the usual deck of fifty-two. The court cards are not Knaves and Queens, but personalities of history and mythology ranging from Cupid and Proserpine to Wat Tyler and the Pharaoh of the Bible. But the Kings were kept, because they were the cards which directed the questions. The suits were also retained, but the cards were not covered by the pips, because the space was required for further fortune-telling matter. The odd-pip cards in the pack had a circle with signs of the Zodiac on them, and the even-pip cards each contained thirteen numbered answers as well as a dedication to a popular saint. On each King there were five numbered questions of the type most commonly asked, such as 'Does he really love me?' There was a complicated process by which the enquirer selected a question from the total of twenty carried by the Kings and arrived at an answer from among the 260 on the even-pipped cards. The abstruse directions ended with the re-assuring statement issued on behalf of the Zodiac and Constellations: 'The stars foretell they love you well.'

The nomenclature of cards is interesting, if only as an indication that the Americans, as in so many other instances, are using an old English term and not an Americanism when they speak of a 'deck' of cards. The word 'pips', originally 'peeps', was in use by 1656. On the restoration of Charles II, four years later, when cards became fashionable again after their virtual banning under the Puritans, a pack of cards was called a 'pair' of cards because of European influence, emanating originally from Italy, where the word *paio*, meaning pair, was used collectively for many sets of things, such as a 'pair' of chess. besides a 'pair' of cards. In Queen Elizabeth's time a pack of cards was also called a 'bunch' and in some of Shakespeare's plays it was called a 'deck', a term which endured for a long time in the north of England. Of individual cards, the Nine of Diamonds is called the 'Curse of Scotland'. There are nine different explanations of this nickname, of which the most popular nowadays is that 'the Butcher', the Duke of Cumberland who won the battle of Culloden, scribbled an order that there were to be exemplary reprisals in the massacre of Jacobite prisoners of war and their families when traced around Inverness, using as his medium for despatches the face of the Nine of Diamonds. But it is more likely that the custom began because in the game 'Pope Joan' the Nine of Diamonds is the Pope, and this was a

From *Habits des métiers et professions* by Nicholas de Larmessin (1690), an imaginary card-maker made entirely (apart from his face) from the tools of his trade.

title causing wrathful indignation among the virulent non-Catholics of Scotland. The Ace of Diamonds used to be called in Ireland the 'Earl of Cork', 'because it is the worst ace in the pack, the poorest card, and the Earl of Cork is the poorest nobleman in Ireland'. In Northampton-shire the Queen of Clubs used to be called 'Queen Bess' because Queen Elizabeth I had black hair and dark complexion, though for long she concealed the former under an auburn wig. The word 'trump' was originally spelled 'triumph', as is indicated by an extant sermon delivered by Bishop Latimer at Cambridge, before he was conveyed to Oxford to light the Martyrs' Memorial, when he preached on 'The Card' and spoke of Hearts being his 'triumph' card.

REINE DES ROSES

The Queen of Roses, from a heraldic pack produced
in Lyon in 1692.

7

Educational and Propaganda Cards

THE GLORY OF ENGLAND was her educational cards. But the English did not invent them. In 1507 a set of instructive cards was invented by Dr Thomas Muruer, an active opponent of Martin Luther. The pack was printed at Cracow and called *Chartilidui Logicae* with progressive instruction in the art of reasoning. They had at first been intended for the doctor's personal pupils but their use became very popular for a time. Eventually there was a move against this novelty and the mob – obvious experts in the art of logic – threatened to burn the doctor for having dared to invent them. Cardinal Mazarin designed some *cartes d'instruction* to aid the education of the eight-year-old Louis XIV, who was rather a dull boy before he emerged as the Sun King. Many series of cards illustrating French history were later produced in France over the following centuries and the other popular subject for education by the dealing of cards was heraldry. These were taken up in England in the seventeenth century. But the English innovation was the production of cards teaching geography and these were speedily copied in Italy and other countries. These English cards were first published in 1675, and, although they bore the nominal emblems of the suits, by far the most space was annexed for information. The instructions read: 'The four suits are the four parts of England. The thirteen northern counties are clubs, the western are spades, the eastern are hearts, and the southern are diamonds. In each card you have a map of the county with the chief towns and rivers, a compass for the bearings and a scale of mensuration. There is also given the length, breadth and circumference of each county, the latitude of the chief city or town, and its distance from London . . . There is also the road from London to each city or town, the great roads are drawn with a double line, the other roads with a single line, as also the hills and other remarks.' This pack was speedily reprinted and later extended to cover England and Wales. Very soon there was an issue of a geographical guide to the world, with hand-coloured medallion portraits of the rulers of the territories. The enthusiasm for this sort of instruction led to the issue of cards intended for biased instruction, or propaganda. In 1679 there was issued 'The horrid Popish Plot, lively represented in a pack of cards' which was really much more a series of artistically polished engravings than the crude comic strip which one might have expected. Accomplished satire was issued in playing-card form with the pack called 'Marlborough's Victories' – a sort of *Private Eye* view of contemporary history in the light of the proliferating political scandals of the day. This trend went even farther when the scandal of the South Sea Bubble broke to the rueful remorse of so many who had lost their money, and in this still artistically accomplished series people were portrayed as making their comments in bubbles issuing from their mouths, a device which the satiric cartoonists of the day speedily popularised. An interesting set of 'educational' cards is the pack containing the lyrics and airs of *The Beggar's Opera*, published in fact many years after its first production. There were packs of cards reprinting proverbs, Aesop's *Fables*, and the basics of arithmetic. In the nineteenth century astronomy, history, and even law-court procedure was taught to children through card games. And the list of educational packs of cards, all of them now collector's pieces, ended where it had started in Luther's day with an exposition of the Bible.

The best propaganda defence of cards, which is in itself adequately educational as a mnemonic, is the famous broadsheet entitled *Cards Spiritualized: or the Soldier's Almanac, Bible and Prayer Book* which circulated for scores of years during the nineteenth century. It reads:

Richard Middleton, a soldier, attending divine service with the rest of the regiment at a church in Glasgow, instead of pulling out a Bible, like his brother soldiers, to find the parson's text, spread a pack of cards before him. This singular behaviour did not long pass unnoticed, both by the clergyman and the serjeant of the company to which he belonged; the latter in particular requested him to put up the cards, and on his refusal, conducted him after church before the Mayor, to whom he preferred a formal complaint of

The declension of Latin for French students is the
subject of this card from a pack produced around
1640. The elegance of the design suggests the work of
a talented artist.

The Four of Scorpions, from a 16th century German
educational pack, is crowded with obscure symbols.

Richard's indecent behaviour during divine service. 'Well, soldier!' (said the Mayor) 'what excuse have you for this strange scandalous behaviour? If you can make any apology, or assign any reason for it, it's well: if you cannot, assure yourself that I will cause you, without delay, to be severely punished for it.' 'Since your honour is so good,' replied Richard, 'I will inform you. I have been eight days on march, with a bare allowance of sixpence a day, which your honour will surely allow is hardly sufficient to maintain a man in meat, drink, washing, and other necessaries that consequently he may want, without a Bible, Prayer Book, or any other good book.' On saying this, Richard drew out his pack of cards, and presenting one of the aces to the Mayor, continued his address to the magistrate as follows:

'When I see an Ace, may it please your honour, it reminds me that there is only one God; and when I look upon a Two or a Three, the former puts me in mind of the Father and the Son, and the latter of Father, Son and Holy Ghost. A Four calls for remembrance the four Evangelists, Matthew, Mark, Luke and John. A Five the five wise Virgins who were ordered to trim their lamps; there were ten, indeed, but five, your worship may remember, were wise, and five were foolish. A Six, that in six days God created heaven and earth. A Seven, that on the seventh day he rested from all that he had made. An Eight, of the eight righteous persons preserved from the deluge: *viz.*, Noah and his wife with his three sons and their wives. A Nine, of the nine lepers cleansed by our Saviour; there were ten, but one only returned to offer his tribute of thanks. And a Ten, of the ten commandments that God gave Moses on Mount Sinai, on the two tables of stone.' He took the Knave and put it aside. 'When I see the Queen, it puts me in mind of the Queen of Sheba, who came from the furthermost parts of the world to hear the wisdom of Solomon, for she was as wise a woman as he a man, for she brought fifty boys and fifty girls, all clothed in girls' apparel to show before King Solomon, for him to test which were boys and which were girls, – but he could not until he called for water to wash themselves; the girls washed up to their elbows, and the boys only up to the wrists of their hands, so King Solomon told by that. And when I see the King it puts me in mind of the Great King of Heaven and Earth, which is God Almighty; and likewise his Majesty King George the Fourth, to pray for him.' 'Well,' said the Mayor, 'you have given a good description of all the cards except one, which is lacking.' 'Which is that?' said the soldier. 'The Knave', said the Mayor.

'If your honour will not be angry with me,' returned Richard, 'I can give you the same satisfaction on that as any in the pack?' 'No', said the Mayor. 'Well,' returned the soldier, 'the greatest knave that I know is the serjeant who brought me before you.' 'I don't know,' said the Mayor, 'whether he be the greatest knave or no,'but I am sure he is the greatest fool.'

The soldier then continued as follows: 'When I count the number of dots in a pack of cards, there are 365, – so many days as there are in the year. When I count how many cards there are in a pack, I find there are 52, – so many weeks are there in a year. When I reckon how many tricks are won by a pack, I find there are 13, – so many [lunar] months are there in a year. So that this pack of cards is both Bible, Almanack, and Prayer book to me.'

The Mayor called his servants, ordered them to entertain the soldier well, gave him a piece of money, and said that he was the cleverest fellow he had ever heard in his life.

8

The Rules of Fortune-Telling Outside the Tarot Pack

THE TRADITIONAL CONVENTIONS are as follows: a man of very fair complexion is represented by the King of Diamonds; a woman by the Queen of the same suit. Persons of less fair complexion, according to sex, by the King and Queen of Hearts. A man and woman of very dark complexion are represented by the King and Queen of Spades, while those not quite so dark are denoted by Clubs. If a married woman consults the cards, the King of her own colour represents her husband, whether he is fair or dark, and vice versa if the cards are consulted by a married man. Lovers, whether they are recognised or hope to be contracted, are always represented by cards of their particular colours, and all cards when representing persons lose their normal significance. But there are exceptions: a widow, no matter how fair she is, can be represented only by the Queen of Spades; a man wearing uniform must be represented by the King of Diamonds – but the dress of a policeman is not considered uniform. The Ace of Hearts denotes the house of the person consulting Fate. The Ace of Clubs signifies a letter. The Ace of Diamonds means a wedding ring. The Ace of Spades is sickness and death. The Knave of Hearts is a selfish and deceitful fraud. The Knave of Spades is a lawyer, and a person to be avoided. The Knave of Clubs is a sincere friend, but of very touchy temper. In all instances, however, the Knaves signify the thoughts of their respective Kings and Queens, and consequently the thoughts of the persons whom those Kings and Queens represent in accordance with their complexion; and when doing so they lose their normal significance. Generally speaking, Diamonds and Hearts are more fortunate than Spades and Clubs. Several Diamonds coming together signify the receipt of money. A concourse of Clubs foretells drunkenness and debauchery, and a number of Spades together indicate disappointment.

The Kings and Queens, besides representing colour, have a private significance of their own. The King of Diamonds is quick to anger but easily appeased, while the Queen is fond of gaiety and is of rather a coquettish disposition. The King of Hearts is slow to anger, but when he is in a passion he is appeased with great difficulty; he is good-natured, but rather obstinate; his Queen, however, is a model of sincere affection, devotion and prudence. The King of Spades is so ambitious that in matters of love or business he is much less scrupulous than he ought to be, while his Queen is a person not to be provoked with impunity, never forgetting an injury and having a considerable spice of malice in her disposition. The King and Queen of Clubs are everything that can be desired: he is honourable, true and affectionate; she is agreeable, genteel and witty.

The interpretations of the minor cards are as follows:

DIAMONDS:
Ten. Wealth. Honourable success in business.
Nine. A roving disposition, combined with successful adventure in foreign lands.
Eight. A happy marriage, though perhaps late in life.
Seven. Satire. Scandal.
Six. Early marriage succeeded by widowhood.
Five. Unexpected (though generally good) news.
Four. An unfaithful friend. A secret betrayed.
Trey. Domestic quarrels. Trouble. Unhappiness.
Deuce. A clandestine engagement. A card of caution.

HEARTS:
Ten. Health and happiness, with many children.
Nine. Wealth, and a good position in society.
Eight. Fine clothes. Mixing in good society. Invitations to balls, theatres, parties.
Seven. Good friends.
Six. Honourable courtship.
Five. A present.
Four. Domestic troubles caused by jealousy.

The Four of Diamonds, from a transformation pack by
Olivatte, 1828. The numerals are cleverly worked into
the design.

Les animaux savans

The Nine of Spades, entitled 'The Clever Animals',
from '*Cartes à Rire*', attributed to Baron Louis Atthalin
in the 19th century.

Trey. Poverty, shame and sorrow, the result of imprudence. A card of
  caution.
Deuce. Success in life, and a happy marriage attained by virtuous
  discretion.

SPADES:

Ten. Disgrace, crime, imprisonment. Death on the scaffold. A card of
  caution.
Nine. Grief, ruin, sickness, death.
Eight. Great danger from imprudence. A card of caution.
Seven. Unexpected poverty through the death of a relative.
Six. A child. To the unmarried, a card of caution.
Five. Great danger from giving way to bad temper. A card of caution.
Four. Sickness.
Trey. Tears. A removal by land.
Deuce. A removal.

CLUBS:

Ten. Unexpected wealth through the death of a relative.
Nine. Danger through drunkenness. A card of caution.
Eight. Danger from covetousness. A card of caution.
Seven. A prison. Danger from the opposite sex. A card of caution.
Six. Competence by honourable industry.
Five. A happy, though not wealthy, marriage.
Four. Misfortunes through caprice or inconstancy. A card of caution.
Trey. Quarrels. It also has a reference to time, signifying three years,
  three months, three weeks, or three days (what we call in the
  craft 'three somethings'), and denotes that a person will be
  married more than once.
Deuce. Disappointment. Vexation.

The general mode of operation is that the person consulting Fortune,
after shuffling the cards, cuts them into three parts. The fortune-teller
takes up the parts, lays them out one by one face upward on the table,
in rows of nine save the last. Every ninth card has a portentous import,
while each nine consecutive cards form a separate combination,
complete in itself; yet, like a word in a sentence, no more than a
fractional part of the grand scroll of Fate. Moreover, each card,
something like the octaves in music, has a particular bearing on the
ninth card from it, and these ninth cards form in themselves peculiar
combinations of nines though part of the general whole. The Nine of

[125]

The Queen of Clubs, represented by Cleopatra, in a
pack of cards designed for Colonel Atthalin, an officer
in the court of Louis Philippe, *c.* 1832.

Hearts is the wish card, and after the fortune has been told the cards are well shuffled and cut, the cut card being particularly remembered. The pack is again well shuffled and cut into three heaps, each of which is taken up and examined separately. If the wish card, the Nine of Hearts, is found in any of these heaps near the representative card of the person whose fortune is being told, the wish will be gratified sooner or later, according to the relative positions of the cards. If the Nine of Spades, Deuce of Clubs, or another very unlucky card is in the same heap, the gratification of the wish is doubtful or will be unduly delayed according to the number of unlucky cards. But if the card cut is in the same heap, the evil effect of the opposing unlucky cards will be substantially decreased.

STOCKTON - BILLINGHAM
LIBRARY
TECHNICAL COLLEGE

A NOTE ON THE TYPEFACE

This book was composed on the Monotype in Baskerville, Series 169, a face based upon the designs of John Baskerville (1707–75). The wide letter forms of the Dutch and English Old faces were retained in English Transitional and Modern faces, but it was Baskerville who was the first to move in the direction of vertical stress. The face's generous proportions make it one of the most handsome and legible of designs. The width of the letters counteracts the vertical pull of the stress, and the open counters and clean, crisp lines make it possible to print well on a wide variety of papers. The italic is narrower than the roman, and its design clearly shows the influence of contemporary handwriting. The Monotype cutting was undertaken in 1923.